PRISCILLA WACHIRA

Seated

My Journey To Becoming

GREAT BOOKS

First published by GREAT Books 2021

Copyright © 2021 by Priscilla Wachira

All rights reserved. No part of this publication may be reproduced, stored or transmitted in any form or by any means, electronic, mechanical, photocopying, recording, scanning, or otherwise without written permission from the publisher. It is illegal to copy this book, post it to a website, or distribute it by any other means without permission.

Priscilla Wachira asserts the moral right to be identified as the author of this work.

Scripture quotations marked TPT are from The Passion Translation®. Copyright © 2017, 2018 by Passion & Fire Ministries, Inc. Used by permission. All rights reserved. ThePassionTranslation.com.

Scripture quotations marked (NIV) are taken from the Holy Bible, New International Version®, NIV®. Copyright © 1973, 1978, 1984, 2011 by Biblica, Inc.™ Used by permission of Zondervan. All rights reserved worldwide. www.zondervan.comThe "NIV" and "New International Version" are trademarks registered in the United States Patent and Trademark Office by Biblica, Inc.™

Scripture quotations marked NLT are taken from the Holy Bible, New Living Translation, copyright © 1996, 2004, 2015 by Tyndale House Foundation. Used by permission of Tyndale House Publishers, Inc., Carol Stream, Illinois 60188. All rights reserved.

"Scripture quotations taken from the Amplified® Bible (AMP), Copyright © 2015 by The Lockman Foundation. Used by permission. www.lockman.org"

First edition

Cover art by Roy Kamau
Editing by Mary Wachira
Front Cover Photo by Cecilie Wachira
Back Cover Photo by Kendall Nicole Studios

Contents

Introduction	iv
1 The Examined Life	1
2 The Beginning of My Becoming	12
3 The Wakeup Call	21
4 The Enemy to Vulnerability	29
5 And So I Waited	36
6 The Difficulty in Vulnerability	43
7 The Change I Needed	51
8 The Change I Believe In	56
9 Alone with God; Lessons from My Wait	68
10 The Art of Living; Being Seated	79
Notes	95
About the Author	97

Introduction

Greetings, dear reader.

I am glad you chose to pick up this book and glance into its pages with sheer curiosity about what lies within. Allow me to introduce myself. My name is Priscilla Wachira. I enjoy sunny Saturdays, crisp, clean spaces, Whataburger patty melts, Chinese food, and most of all, empowering people to revel in their uniqueness.

You are probably wondering what exactly this book is about and why it is titled Seated: My Journey to Becoming and whether I will get to the point already. Indeed, I will but, before we begin I would like to ask you a favor.

This will require your **undivided attention** and before I get into the details of what exactly that means, join me as we travel back in time together.

I want you to recall a memory that left you feeling disconnected, isolated, and unaware of who you truly were.

> *Now, pause right there.*

I know you may be thinking hold up, wait a minute. We haven't even hit the first chapter, and you're already in my personal space asking me to journey with you? No, ma'am. I do not feel like traveling, especially when there's a pandemic going on. *(For those that may read this later in time, I am pretty sure what I am referring to is in your history books, if not Google Covid-19)*

> *Resume.*

I know that asking you to journey to such a time and place may sound off-putting, but flow with me here and ask yourself these questions:

- *When I pictured that memory, what did I feel?*
- *Did I **push through** the emotions and **process the** whole experience?*
- *Did I let it flash quickly through my mind without giving a thought to the emotions?*
- *What did I do?*

I am asking these questions because such adverse (negative) experiences and the emotions attached to them are normally **pushed past or forgotten as a form of resilience**. According to Socioemotional Selectivity Theory[1], as people age, they become more motivated to **reserve** positive experiences while **separating** themselves from negative ones[2]. As a result, these experiences lack the mental and emotional space needed to address them properly.

This is due to the consistent denial or avoidance (e.g *suppression*) as discussed in this book (more details in Chapter 1 titled *The Examined Life*). From there, the mind begins to compute these reactions as positive emotions and stores them in a special folder for use when the need arises.

When a situation presents itself, the brain produces the necessary verbal responses to keep an individual in a state of "balance" as they address the negative situation or emotion. Examples of common phrases I've heard that people use to avoid dealing with tough situations and emotions are:

- *Learn to be more rational*
- *Emotions make you look sloppy*
- *Get over it*
- *Don't catch feelings*
- *Just move on*
- *Forgive but don't forget*
- *The hustle keeps you going*
- *It could not be me, but you can*
- *What does not kill you, makes you stronger*

With all of these phrases in mind, I want to mention the favor proposed earlier. I would like to invite you to *journey through the process* of **becoming** with me.

Before we expound on the meaning of becoming and its relevance to this book, keep in mind that it takes greater courage to surrender and acknowledge the negative moments in your life than the strength needed to hold it all in for the sake of "balance"

In order to acknowledge these adverse experiences throughout our lives openly and authentically, an act of surrender is required…

You might be asking well, what kind of surrender? It sounds intense. Well, you are correct.

This form of surrender comes from deep within and is very specific to you and your calling in life.

For me, it was the cry that I had been aching to release for a long time but I did not know how to do it authentically; even when I thought I was it was fifty percent surrender, fifty percent holding back, in case the situation backfired on me.

I was always in the defense, ready to aim and then put my walls back up. My cry was heavy, painful, and deep, but it was not done hoping. Your cry is special and unique to you, and it can consist of many different kinds of tears: happy, joyful, sad, glad, relieved, mad, etc.

Consequently, this cry is what leads you to a stillness within like no other, mentally and spiritually.

God is able to take all of our sorrows and turn them into something good. The pain you feel is just a part of the journey and I am confident that it is what keeps us surrendered to what matters most, **becoming** who God has called us to be.

God's goodness overrides everything that we could ever face in life, and because of that constant promise, we can find rest at his feet. The amazing Tasha Cobbs said it best in her song titled *"Forever at Your Feet"*:

> *"And I will be seated at your feet*
> *To worship at your feet*
> *I will be right here at your feet*

Forever."

Therefore, the more we stay seated at his feet, the easier it is to maintain our surrender.

> *Author's Note: The courage required to begin, and sustain you is fueled by endless amounts of empathy and vulnerability for yourself and others. As you recollect the memories discussed earlier, remember to pause and reflect on your emotions as well. In the same way, take in the lessons you missed, no matter how hard they may be to accept and flourish in that space of growth. While doing all this, you will notice yourself becoming a different person altogether.*

The once dormant things in your heart will begin to resurrect with passion. Your eyes will begin to perceive hope to see your dreams fulfilled again, and most of all, your voice will begin to quicken with courage as you declare your story. Not just any story, but the story of how **you** *journeyed through the process of becoming.*

For those who are like me and are thinking, "okay this is heavy and good, but I need a simple format to get me through." Well, I am glad you asked because I have formed an equation that will be your compass through this book

$$\frac{\text{Courage}}{\text{Empathy} + \text{Vulnerability}} = \text{Becoming}$$

1. **You** cannot go through an experience that caused you great mental and emotional discomfort without the **courage** to start.
2. Once you have started, you will need **empathy and vulnerability** to sustain you.
3. These three terms form a **safe space (cocoon)** for you to **flourish** in the growth process and once you can flourish safely, you evolve **(become)** a different person or better yet the person you were destined to be.

In closing, my humble prayer is that God will reveal and download the moments in your life that He wants to heal. I pray that His power will help **push you through the memories, discover the lessons you might have overlooked**, and **continue to flourish in the healing process** as you move towards *becoming* the man/woman He created you to be.

Throughout this safari (trip) together, remember that "becoming is never giving up on the idea that there's **more growing** to be done."- Michelle Obama.

So, take a deep breath—hold it, release, and know that we are in this together.

1

The Examined Life

It was a calm, dawning day on October 14th, 1990, in a town lying northeast of Nakuru, Kenya called Nyahururu (Nya-hu-ru-ru). The town derived its name from the Maasai word ***e-naiwurruwurr***, meaning waterfall, windy, and/or place of storms, located in Laikipia County.[3]

It was there that I made my thundering debut into the world.

"Surprise! She's here!"

My aunt Tabby (Tabitha) announced to my dad who, as per the stories I hear, ran non-stop from work at the local high school where he was teaching to the hospital room. On the day I was born, the attending doctor and his team were in shock from start to finish. Apparently, they had never seen such a fast-paced and smooth delivery process. Even to my mom, it was as if I had one goal in mind and no complications would hold me back; so, I pushed her—not the other way around.

As I grew, this description of how I came into this world fiercely resonated with me. I turned out to be quite the animated little girl—ready to play, laugh, lead, speak up, and most of all, take on any challenge the world's playground held.

On the flip side, being the toughest of my two older siblings distressed my mother at times. For example, I chipped my tooth once and instead of crying,

I walked up, flashed a huge, beaming smile, and excitedly shouted *"Ta-Da!"* My brother and sister were well reserved and already had the rule book in hand memorized from birth! My brother, being the oldest, always erred on the side of caution in order to maintain discipline since he was left in charge most of the time.

It was this discipline and focus that drove him to become the mighty man of valor that he is in society today. Many look up to my brother, and it is obvious that his journey to becoming was not easy as the eldest, but he has continued to pave the way and empower us to aim higher. My sister, on the other hand, erred on the side of caution primarily for her own mental wellness.

Picture this: My mother would leave her on the couch in the morning and find her seated in the same spot by the time she returned in the evening. In sum, she preferred to mentally explore rather than physically put herself in such a challenge first.

Consequently, her reading and analytical skills grew to become her forte and to this day, my sister can easily plan out an event of a thousand plus in her head in one hour at most. During this planning phase, she has already examined the room in her head, explored all possibilities, and outcomes knowing exactly what she will need to succeed.

Talk about impressive and it's all a result of learning how to literally be still and **seated** long enough to examine the possibilities around us. The world is our canvas and the pallet of ideas is endless; anything is literally possible if you give yourself the time and space to examine it well. Thank you, Elizabeth, for that lesson.

I, on the contrary, did not want to be still or seated for that matter. I wanted to immerse myself physically into the world around me so much that I fell into a sewage river once while my dad was preaching at a church service held on the city lawn and had to wade through a crowd of people to find my mom. You are probably thinking, that poor lady. Let me tell you, God Particularly handcrafted her to handle my rambunctiousness and so much more. I owe her a lot. *This one's for you mom.*

Although I grew up as the poster-child for being young, wild, and free, I struggled to find a place that I belonged to, instead of just passing through. My father raised me to see the world through a lens of endless possibilities, like a long, massive buffet table lined with a plethora of cuisines ready to satisfy anyone who took a seat, and although that sounded quite inviting, I always wondered whether there was a seat for me at this table.

Aside from outdoor activities, my parents fostered an environment that encouraged candid perspectives of the world and its various systems of thought. My father's graduate studies focused on religion, ethics, and philosophy. This meant that he made sure we learned to articulate and question ideas clearly, take in different world views, customs, and religions. Most of all, he taught us to **surrender to the process of becoming.** He believed that by empowering us to have such mindsets, we would successfully discover and thrive in our life's purpose.

Even with such tremendous support and encouragement, there were still moments of extreme doubt and constant periods of having an identity crisis. I lost count of how many times I fought the nagging temptation to just run away from the life and family I was given. I longed to create a new foundation on my own, where no one knew who I was so I could *"breathe in freely."*

You're probably asking, 'what do you mean to breathe in freely?' Allow me to lay the foundation of how I grew up clearly to you, from there I think the answers may start to form.

I was brought up in the Akorino faith and my father was a well-known pastor in most parts of the country for debunking the stereotypes that the Kenyan society had formed of the Akorino. Let's take a quick walk down history lane, shall we?

> *Author's Note: Allow me to give you some historical background of the Akorino people.*

"The Akorino started appearing in the middle of the 1920s. Those were very difficult years for the Agikuyu people and other communities in Kenya. By 1920, Kenya had been declared a British colony, and Kenyans were forced to carry kipande, to work in white settlers' farms, to pay taxes and to adhere to foreign religious beliefs and governance structures.

This made the entire community dissatisfied with the colonial regime and saw the birth of many anti-mission and anti-government movements that focused on liberating the country from their colonial masters. This was given impetus by the return of soldiers from World War One who told the people what violence meant.

Akorino, unlike other independent churches, came up as a peace movement. They reacted towards the colonial aggression by withdrawal and rejection. They preached a non-violent opposition of unjust colonial policies that discriminated against and exploited Africans.

They refused to carry kipande, to be counted during censuses, to pay taxes, to take their children to missionary schools or hospitals, and to be employed in settlers' farms. They also abstained from buying colonial industrial goods from the shops, to eat or drink from plates and cups, or to travel by vehicles." (Gachanga, 2021)[4]

The Akorino Church is an African Pentecostal church. It is one of the African Indigenous Churches (AIC's) that grew out of indigenous leadership. The history of the church is deeply rooted within the hardships faced by Kenyans who struggled against colonial dictatorship. Likewise, religious and cultural influences from the western that were carefully arranged by missionary groups.

The church developed Pentecostal teachings and practices without the influence of western Pentecostalism that arose from the Azusa Revival. "As a movement of protest against western imperialism, the Arathi also known as prophets who founded the Akorino Church, exhibited Pentecostal practices like speaking in tongues, prophesying, healing and among others." (Waigwa, 2007)[5]

As a result, we lived under a constant spotlight and still do now; the difference today is, I have learned to embrace it, not shy away from it.

Additionally, I have the confidence to say to you and the whole world that these two factors, being raised Akorino and the daughter of a well-known Akorino preacher who was unashamed to speak the truth about our people, paved a pivotal path to my becoming.

Although, back then both factors were deeply burdensome and nothing to celebrate about. Likewise, they etched a deep wound in my heart and thus created the immense desire to live a life of solitude, unknown in the shadows.

No matter how hard I tried to avoid my thoughts or suppress my emotions, and act like everything was okay; my parents' resounding reminder of what it meant to live an examined life always played in the back of my head.

Now, are you ready for a philosophy lesson? Did you think it would come to this? *Well, let us pause the story time and take a quick detour.*

Socrates was a philosopher from Athens, Greece born in the year 469 B.C.E. He shaped the cultural and intellectual advancement of the world that, without him, history would be

widely different. Likewise, he is best known for the creation of the Socratic method of question and answer. Through this method, he confessed that he was ignorant, or better said, he was *aware* of his **lack of knowledge**. It was this claim that coined the statement: *"The unexamined life is not worth living, for human beings."*[6]

This declaration professed that living a life under the labels of society, a group of people and their rules, in a continuous routine without questioning your identity or life's purpose was not a life worth fulfilling. Thus, a thorough introspection of the mind and emotions was and still is vital to understanding one's personal imprint in this world.

Don't get me wrong, this is not a charge to completely terminate one's life socially, no, that would be a far-reaching assumption. On the contrary, it is the relentless nudge or small, beckoning voice in the back of your subconscious that inspires you to step forth from the mundane. It is the heart-pounding, palms sweating, dry throat desire that empowers you to ask yourself, *'Is this the life I deserve?'*

It's the voice those dear to you have probably been guiding you towards all along. Every time you decide to address this calling within, your mind and body go numb. Frozen in what seems like an eternity, inches from the edge, paralyzed by the fear of *'what will they think? What will I think?'*

You back away slowly and snug your way back into the familiar comfort zone. In other words, you know that you're meant for something bigger, yet you struggle to comprehend what it is without judging what it looks, sounds, or even feels like. You even train your mind and emotions to suppress the grandiose vision of what others can see you becoming.

Sometimes, when you see the vision clearly and it does not connect with you internally, it leaves you questioning why it matters if there is no passion within. This distasteful cycle leaves you feeling drained spiritually and mentally as you wander, seeking solace from this ever-so-familiar confusion. However, even in the mental/emotional chaos, you find peace in knowing that there are voices that genuinely desire to see you blossom in infinite ways.

On the other hand, there are other voices that seem to know you in and out, but they come bearing alternate choices. These voices enter your life from time to time to check in on you. For example, they come in at random times with a text saying *"long time no see"* or *"hey there stranger"* text and at times you fight the urge to respond. For a few minutes, you engage, but then minutes turn to hours and you find yourself mentally rerouted from point A to God only knows where. Also, it is as if these voices always know when you are about to make a big move, so they swoop in smoothly and distract you from taking the next big step.

Now, let me clarify here, that for some, these check-ins are necessary and most of the time, they do provide clarity through a fresh voice. Perhaps, it is the timing and season that are not right. Although the idea is good, the blueprint for executing the goal needs to be re-visited or thought through clearly. Overall, these voices assist in drawing a clearer picture than what you had initially brought to the drawing board.

All that said, you, my dear, must be discerning of the intent behind their voices because some speak to lead you towards truth and others towards confusion. Some are cheering you towards the leap, while others want to keep you on safe ground. Those that lead you towards confusion do so through a process in which they attribute their own individual positive or negative characteristics and opinions to you, e.g projecting. This behavior is often a form of protection where any unpleasant or inappropriate impulses, stressors, thoughts, emotions, or duties are attributed to others. (American Psychological Association, 2021)[7]

Sometimes these projections are well-thought-out and executed consciously, meaning the individual is "perceiving, apprehending, or noticing with a degree of controlled thought or observation." Now, refer back to the word I shared back in the introduction section called Suppression. This requires, "the conscious intentional exclusion from the consciousness of a thought or feeling." The opposite of this is behavior that is subconscious, meaning it is "existing in the mind but not immediately available to consciousness."[8]

Collectively, these three terms work together to form defense mechanisms for avoiding negative thoughts and emotions. In addition to, a sense of immediacy and reward, whether mental or physical. The reward(s) act as binoculars that focus on more pleasant recollections and avoid the unpleasant ones as I mentioned during the introduction according to the Socioemotional Selectivity Theory.[9]

In sum, an individual who is unable to properly address their thoughts or emotions has the liberty to **move through** the unpleasant memories as they wish based on the defensive mechanisms they operate consciously or subconsciously.

Now you may think 'this is not fair because what if this is all the individual has ever known as a means to survive? To them, the term defense mechanism may mean nothing, but proper behavior to them.' Yes, you are right and studies have shown how this way of thinking and behaving is formed.

According to Baumeister, Dale, and Sommer, "a particular crisis in self-perception may arise when an internal or external event occurs that clearly **violates** the preferred view of self. In such cases, it is necessary for the self to have some mechanism or process to defend itself against the threatening implications of this event. Such processes are commonly called defense mechanisms."[10] All of these mechanisms are rooted in the experiences we face or have faced in the past.

For example, I grew up hearing that I was a go-getter and came into this world ready to achieve all that life had to offer. However, the more I entertained voices that spoke otherwise and put myself in situations that "violated" the view I had of myself… enough was enough and I had to decide whether to stay comfortable living an unexamined life or push through the discomfort. In my decision to push through, the mechanisms I once learned to operate in to move forward instead became limiting and weighty.

Altogether, you must learn that some voices want to distract you for as long as they can and will do it effectively, innocently, and without fault on their part. They find peace knowing you may never accomplish your goal or walk in your purpose as long as they have access to *speak* into your life.

They will work hard to make sure any form of self-examination is redirected by taking on the role of being a safe space for you, especially without even being asked. This invites projections of their own will into your mind and heart.

Here are some phrases to look out for that I heard when I shared my personal ambitions with the wrong voices:

- *"That is crazy"*
- *"It is not possible"*
- *"How will you even start, you do not have the means to do so"*
- *"People won't fall for that, you are crazy"*
- *"Go ahead, I will be here waiting to say: I told you so..."*
- *"Only you P, only you."*
- *"Pris, dream harder, you will make it."*
- *"That's nice,"* followed by awkward silence and subject change...

As mentioned, the mistake I made as a young child was allowing these voices to overpower my family's voice. At that age, my family was the only thing I knew and could lean on. So, to solicit input from people who didn't even know what my favorite subject in school was wasn't the right way to go.

Some of you may be wondering, 'don't children need guidance more than anyone else to properly understand themselves? And doesn't this improve their mental/emotional well-being? It does take a community to raise a child, yes? So, why limit the community's voice, especially if it is good advice?'

You are correct it does and these voices do impact their social and mental development advancement into adulthood.

According to the National Scientific Council on The Developing Child, The foundations of social competence that are developed in the first five years are linked to emotional well-being and affect a child's ability to functionally adapt in school and to form successful relationships throughout life. As a person develops into adulthood, these same social skills are essential for the formation of lasting friendships and intimate relationships, effective parenting, the ability to hold a job and work well with others, and for becoming a contributing member of a community.[11]

Because these voices are highly fundamental in shaping the child's mental, emotional and social skills, they need to be voices that, first, provide safety and give clarity where correction and guidance are necessary.

As my father's name grew, so did the spotlight and platform around us as a family unit. I respected the platform, but actively hid from its reflections because of the voices that followed. These voices were confident of my future career. In turn, they also expected me to respect and do as I was told. And in doing so, they did not hesitate to correct my personality as they were "molding" me to be the best and wanted to be remembered in the process. When news of my family's move to the Americas became known, the voices only grew louder.

I recall being told to become a nanny or an elementary school teacher and that doing so was a great honor to the community. The highest achievement attributed to me was to graduate with my first degree "at least", so I could be an office assistant in the Americas.

You must know that I did not know much about America, or what was ahead of me. I did not know what school we'd attend or even which town we were to live in. What I did know was that these voices would soon fade away.

Please understand that it was not that I looked down upon the professions they suggested... As a matter of fact, I considered them as my top few choices because of the amazing teachers and nannies I had growing up. Nevertheless, the comments that followed their suggestions left me feeling smaller than I already was. And I felt guilty for compromising with people, who I knew would not be a part of my journey, so I rejected the whole process with my entire being.

In the midst of all the chatter, the only two things I was certain of were that I did not know who I was, and I no longer had space to take on any more confusion dressed in advice.

Eventually, I started questioning those who suggested a career path for me and why they thought this was a good fit for me. Through their long-winded answers with no end and dismissal of my understanding, it became clear as they stood shocked that a child was questioning an adult.

I was expected to submit to their knowledge without seeing beyond what I knew I could become. At times I hoped someone would advise me to be a pastor or a university teacher like my father, but their answers were always the same over and over—wordy without a clear explanation or direct truth. At times I thought, *'is it because I was a girl?'*

I remember my dad telling my sister and me that we could become anything we wanted to be in the world. With enough faith, focus, and determination, anything was possible and attainable.

I was raised around women who shattered glass ceilings and made a name for themselves in society. What I failed to question was what it took them to get there, and looking back, I should have. Maybe their answers would have created a sense of fear within me. Either way, I am glad I learned on my own the limitations that society sets on women from an early age.

The outcome was that I began to discern who was projecting and who was uplifting me, as should you. There are three takeaways from those experiences listed below to ensure that your mental and emotional wellness is prioritized above other people's voices.

1. I agreed not to share my ideas or feelings openly with anyone and allowed my humor to take precedence as a cover for me.
2. If I needed to share my feelings with anyone, I did it from a place of intellectualism and made sure my words were clearly articulated.
3. I steered clear from any situations that would cause me to appear weak in any way possible.

Keep in mind, I made these decisions at the age of five and although they seemed right to me at the time, I knew that they would not sustain me forever.

Seasons eventually change, as well as people, and ultimately, I would change. Here are some questions to consider.

What are some decisions you remember making at a young age? How did you feel making them? Do you remember the exact time and place you were in when you did so? Also, which voices spoke the truth to you? Which ones spoke confusion and lastly, how did you learn to discern the difference?

In the next chapter, I will share with you three key principles that acted as guides to forming relationships in a healthy way.

2

The Beginning of My Becoming

Have you ever gone through a season of feeling empty with no direction or answer regarding who you are or what you have been created for? You know that feeling is there, but you never take the time to process it because it doesn't feel authentic when you try.

I mean, where do you start? Do you journal, go for a walk, cry, run, etc? Sometimes, you feel like a computer that has just glitched out in the memory-activating system or something like that, if that's even a name. Overall, you feel robotic and apathetic to the world, your own thoughts, and your emotions.

Psychology helped bring to my attention the voices I had given permission to speak throughout my life and how they guided my decision-making from an early age.

However, the path to discovering that this was my field of interest was quite a rocky one, filled with emotional turmoil and doubt as I navigated the sea of voices in my life.

These voices meant well, and most of them saw the reality of my becoming that I was choosing to avoid or better yet ignorance to me at that point was bliss.

I wanted to become a veterinarian at a young age, simply because of what I saw on television via Nat Geo Wild or any other show that involved caring and doting on precious, wild animals.

To me, that was pure freedom, filled with gorgeous safari sunsets, and views of the Masai Mara that would stretch far and wide.

In sum, I wanted to be free at home and make those wide-open spaces my home. What I did not account for, on the other hand, was the amount of freedom this particular field would bring. Yet, I sat there searching and racking my brain for the key to freedom, when the whole time it was in my hands.

What I am trying to say is this, my fear of the unknown kept me from enjoying the unknown, my assumptions of people and the world itself kept me at bay... When in fact, those assumptions were irrevocably false.

I feared telling my father about my decision to change my major from a field of "heavy science" to one of "soft science," leaving a heavy qualm in my mind. My dear friends who I now have the privilege of calling my sisters to this day encouraged me to let God be God and walk out that chapter of my becoming intentionally and with prayer. *Thank you, ladies, you all know who you are.*

My sisters saw beyond the mountain that was in front of me and reminded me unremittingly that God had already gone ahead and prepared the way for many of these types of conversations to take place in my discovery of self, the only question was: Would I allow Him to take the lead, or would I orchestrate it all by myself?

I am thankful to say that my desire to surrender outweighed my fear of the unknown. Eventually, after multiple conversations, prayers, and support from my family and close friends, I declared myself as a Psychology major.

I encountered new theories, patterns of thinking, and ways of being within this new field of study, and everything seemed to click oh so well! I had found my niche, and from that moment on; no one could tell me anything about Psychology that I did not already know.

I became so comfortable in my own knowledge of the world, that I believed that this one degree made me better than Dr. Phill, Dr. Brene Brown (whom I will reference later), and or any other distinguished expert in the field of social sciences.

I am sure you have felt this way too, I can't be the only one here. Party of one? No!

We have all been in that state of mind where our reality begins to make so much sense to us and for once the walls we used to put up in a fight in exchange for our voice to be heard, can now come down…

We can relax here, take a deep breath and celebrate that we do not have to move for a bit, or defend our actions to anyone else for a little while; surely I am not the only one.

Albeit, the people who push us the hardest, see beyond what we choose to find comfort in. On the contrary, being able to see eye to eye for once if not twice is relaxing, but bracing ourselves for another push towards reality can be frightening; yet deep down we know it is necessary.

Throughout the duration of my undergraduate degree, *I began to realize that my perception of the world and people had been distorted from a young age.* This truth was difficult to swallow and even more difficult to resolve.

Thus, I did what I knew to do best to avoid confrontation: I chose to put up a fight once again to not pursue my masters with facts that I knew did not make sense.

Yet, the unknown was too much to handle and discuss especially for someone who had their lives planned out for them since birth, making such a decision was unnatural to me, so I thought.

The people that I kept ostracizing only wanted the best for me and perceived that but I did not know how to get out of this cycle of blaming my shortcomings onto others (projection) as a method of avoiding (suppression) introspection and taking charge of my actions.

It wasn't until I graduated with my master's and had to face the real challenges of operating as a clinically licensed counselor that this revelation dawned on me.

As a counselor, not every client would openly accept the counseling process right away as they had during my clinical training in school. I had fooled myself into becoming a "skilled" analyst who knew the sequences of everyone's thoughts, emotions, and most of all life stories before they did. In addition, I knew how to compel people into telling me their stories and I could be a safe space as long as it distracted me from dealing with my own pain.

I remember when reality beckoned forcefully and pulled me down from the fantasy world I had created for myself. I was not the little girl, who was able to ask questions that challenged adults to prove their wisdom to me anymore.

Also, at this stage in my life, I thought I knew who I was becoming as I explored deeper into the mental health field. I was doing well in the program, I had found a counseling theory I connected with to guide my counseling sessions and I was making connections in the field to secure an internship position for my clinicals. As far as I was concerned, I was the best counselor in the world and no one could convince me otherwise… I "knew" it all.

One day, I found myself alone without a soul to process the racing thoughts and emotions I was having and it forced me to confront the questions I shrugged off as nonsense while pushing others to answer as a form of growth. I had learned to challenge people to do the hard work that I refused to do myself.

Pause.

Have you ever felt deeply convicted about something you did wrong? You know this whole time you needed to change, but refused to address the main problem until it grew to become unbearable?

Maybe it's that feeling you get when you're alone in the car staring off into space as you eat yet another Big Mac. You promise yourself you wouldn't do it again, and then promise to try again tomorrow, but tomorrow never really comes. If that's not you, it was certainly me and to this day, those questions pierce as hard as they did at first.

Resume.

Then, I did not want to move towards growth. Instead, I used food or shopping to shrug off my thoughts and emotions as a form of coping. At times I would ask myself how or why people felt safe with me when I wasn't even a safe space for myself? Was this true or was it all just make-believe and each person was lying to me like I was that five-year-old girl again?

While the tape of hesitancy to trust people played in my mind, I failed miserably in my attempts to build relationships and maintain them as a way of escaping the deep-rooted issues within. Don't get me wrong, I was able to attract people due to my easy-going nature, but the struggle came when I realized I had to sustain the relationship as well as be vulnerable. *(More on vulnerability later in the book.)*

As this truth dawned on me, everything I thought I knew best about navigating relationships and people went out the window. Although I passed academically as a licensed professional, I was failing miserably in my own life application.

Fixing people became my focus, not helping them heal. Instead of seeing them as they were and learning what they needed to move towards growth, I was the one passing out Band-Aids quickly as a solution. I did not view myself as someone who could be relational without being "clinical."

Thus, this led me to go through bouts of confusion as I struggled to separate person and profession. Although the profession complimented my character as a person, embedding it into my personal life and relationships was unnecessary.

With that frame of thought in mind, what methods of growth have you identified to move you through that space? Have they been successful? For those that have already walked through this battle and overcome congratulations!

How did you work through it and what did you learn through the process? Here is some space to write it out if you'd like.

> *Author's Note: Fixing people is not how the field of psychology or counseling operates. I dare say that if my previous instructors ever find this book, please forgive me. I can proudly say, I made it through and learned to see people clearly as they were, and to this day it's still an ongoing lesson.*

This passion to fix people started from this specific point in my life: intro story

As I went through the growth process, I noticed that we create biases through our experiences or even lack of experiences. Personally, I had formed the narrative of the people I would meet during my career as a counselor and all of them were the same.

According to Merriam Webster biases are "an inclination of temperament or outlook; especially **a personal and sometimes unreasoned judgment;** an instance of such prejudice."

Confronting the experiences you chose to move past, requires you to ask yourself what biases of people and things did I formulate in my mind? As you do this daily, you will begin to view people as they are wholeheartedly allowing them to show you who they truly are not the other way around.

Contrary to what my academic and clinical experience taught me, I viewed everyone as a client who needed my advice whether or not it was solicited. I had convinced myself that rushing to the root cause of people's story, made it easier for them to trust me. Because of that, I began to fulfill a false sense of hope within me that I was creating authentic and long-lasting relationships. I had formed biases of the type of people that needed my "saving" and why I was the only one who could do it.

Little did I know that most of the time, they were fine and it was I who was projecting my experiences onto them as their *rescuer*. I assumed that the only reason people came to me when they were having a tough day or situation was to give them advice; Oh, I was wrong.

I would rush to put on my savior cape, rehearse the words of encouragement that we have all used repeatedly throughout society, to bring immediate relief and alleviate any awkwardness that may arise. From there, I would remedy the wound by placing a verbal Band-Aid on it without actively listening to the person, holding space for them, and calling it quits. I was convinced that I had made everything better, even though I barely scratched the surface.

This need to save people, to always rescue them, and to provide everyone with unsolicited solutions and advice seemed like my way of fulfilling my duty to humanity but deep down it was unfulfilling and it made me fail miserably at forming authentic relationships. In retrospect, making this realization was one of those instances that would have convinced me that there is immense beauty and power in being seated. Unfortunately, it did not.

Now that I am older and wiser, you can learn a few tips from me in the next section, on how to build better relationships that do not involve fixing people.

Just Listen and Remain Seated

Discerning whether or not you need to say something is vital to sustaining relationships. Likewise, if you must say something, ask God for wisdom on what to say, how to say it, or when to say it. In sum, being a sounding board for someone is more important than verbally supporting them. Remember, people begin to heal, the moment they feel heard.

As a result, I made the firm decision to interact with others as well as form relationships guided by these three principles alone.

Number one: You should not assume you know everyone's story or that you can write its conclusion better than they.

Number two: When you are invited into someone's space of vulnerability, it isn't the time to start building flow charts or solution maps for them. Instead, it is a time to **sit still** mentally, actively **listen**, and **hold** space for them.

You may wonder, 'what does it mean to hold space?' I am delighted that you asked. I will go into more detail in chapter 6 titled *The Difficulty in Vulnerability*, so stay tuned.

Number three: Learn to live in a space of self-acceptance. Even if people do not come to you for guidance; it does not mean you are less than or that you do not have anything to offer.

Where your greatest strengths lie, do your greatest weaknesses also. This statement isn't just applied to human tendencies, but even to the forces of nature. For example, the sun has many strengths but if one day it begins to operate above the level or temperature it was created to, we would not survive to tell the tale.

As an individual who is inclined to help in matters of emotional and mental distress; even if it is not directly with the person, knowing my place is more important. Although I possess the gift of communicating with different groups of people, I am still learning how to operate in that space wisely by knowing what to say or not to say, etc.

Therefore, just because you can sense that something is off and needs to be attended to, does not mean it is your duty to come rushing in to save the day. You are capable of assisting in many ways; from afar and still make an impact!

For example, as you are reading this book, I believe that God has been speaking to you regarding your personal growth process, and what that needs to look like, that in itself is a cause for celebration. *Insert dance break here*

Even if the revelation is yet to come, taking an interest in this book with an aim of understanding what it means to surrender to the process of becoming is a change as well. You are positioning your heart for God to do something big in your life, as you allow Him to move you through the painful experiences you used to detour around.

So, with all of that said, If you want to be in a place where others can feel safe coming to you, learn to be a safe space for yourself first. For orders to actively listen to others hold space without trying to fix them, we must harness the discipline to do so with ourselves. Safe spaces are created when those in them know how to properly hold space. I know these terms are used interchangeably, but they have specific meanings that I will expound on later in the chapters.

Now, If that part about being a safe space for yourself first stung internally, you are not alone. I felt the same way when my professor said those exact words to me during the **final clinical check-in** of my master's curriculum. I was more comfortable being a space for someone to be vulnerable, rather than sitting in a space of vulnerability with someone. However, this check-in did just that and it placed me in a space of vulnerability that I could not get out of.

This was only the check-in that most students looked forward to and dreaded at the same time. I think it was the mixture of endings and beginnings all in one. This meeting sifted through all of the past two or so years of coursework and verified if you had met the requirements academically to graduate. It also gave you the permission to sit for the state licensure test that followed graduation… No big deal, right?

I can recollect pacing back and forth that day, as I processed how fast the two years had flown by. Externally I felt ready, but internally the pieces of the puzzle were still being put together. Remember, I knew how to act the part and make myself believe I was a safe space. However, I knew this act would soon run its course and when it did, I told myself I would deal with it then, as you read earlier in the chapter.

When I arrived at the check-in, we discussed our academic work as well as the counseling experience we had gained in our community as a cohort. The conversations were empowering and in the end, we all felt qualified to fulfill the task finally.

This confidence arose in us not just through the words given by our professors, but through the various folders that held our experiences over the past two years. We knew this material not just as students, but as properly, trained clinicians *who would go forth and change the world.*

3

The Wakeup Call

Have you ever been caught in a moment of:

Is this really me?

How did I just do that? (That being whatever big task was ahead of you)

Someone tell me, how did I pull this off?

Was I really awake or did I dream this into fruition?

Well, this was the feeling that overcame me after the clinical check-in mentioned in the previous chapter.

Immediately, I went from *'can I do this?'* to *'Yes I can!'* then to *'what am I doing?'* All my fellow classmates knew that this degree was a big achievement not only for ourselves but also for our loved ones. Most of them had grown up in homes that emphasized achievement as a step towards another great achievement.

Our families created an atmosphere for us to shine, but at times the cost to do so was great mentally, physically, and emotionally. Looking back, I knew my parents meant well and they desired to see their children become the best.

However, in the go-go-go moments, I failed to share my emotional and mental distress with anyone. Instead, I used those moments to highlight the work I was doing and succeeding in. This form of behavior increased my inability to be a safe space for myself because I subconsciously felt as though I did not deserve it.

Additionally, the more I discussed my work, the more I felt undeserving of the opportunities I was granted as an upcoming clinician. I would meet any congratulatory comments with phrases that alluded to teamwork and not being able to accomplish anything without my family or colleagues. Although this was deeply true, I wanted to hide behind the comments and let the people who assisted me emotionally or mentally receive the praise. This never eliminated the conversation but intensified it as the commenter would state that I did do the actual work and that I should be proud of it. I knew that good and well but still did not feel comfortable standing in the spotlight alone.

Trembling with embarrassment and shame, I knew what was happening but in this version of Priscilla, I opted to move past any intense emotions as if they were momentary phases, reflective of the momentary situation.

I was dealing with a bad case of *Imposter Syndrome* but I was incognizant on how to *properly* address it. I knew what it was and how it affected people, yet to confess it as a clinician made it feel worse than it was.

Impostor syndrome (also known as impostor phenomenon, fraud syndrome, perceived fraudulence, or the impostor experience) describes high-achieving individuals who, despite their objective successes, fail to internalize their accomplishments and have persistent self-doubt and fear of being exposed as a fraud or impostor.[12]

People with impostor syndrome struggle with accurately attributing their performance to their actual competence (i.e. they attribute successes to external factors such as luck or receiving help from others and attribute setbacks as evidence of their professional inadequacy).

I learned to hide this struggle well, but one person saw beyond the act and still stayed in that space with me. Once the meeting had ended, I looked for one of my favorite professors, "Dr. M", the one who *saw* me. He knew what I could **become** and was not limited to any perception of it. He was the one who stayed and motivated me to **push through** the painful experiences.

In doing so, he corrected me deeply without hesitation and made sure I understood where his message was coming from; his words were gentle but carried weight even to this day.

Let me pause here to remind you that, when you encounter someone like this in your life, be obedient, as simple as that. Learn to internalize their correction properly and sift through their words for wisdom, for those messages will keep you grounded in times of despair.

Most of the time, I never understood what he meant, but years later that same voice would resound in my head and make perfect sense of the situation I was in. Referring back to the voices and choices… His voice brought tremendous clarity, but at the same time, it kindled the growing pains that I despised. These corrections paved a path that was necessary to becoming a *courageous, empathetic, and most of all vulnerable counselor.* As I stated in the introduction, these three terms taught me to become a safe space for myself.

Dr. M saw beyond the act and reminded me of this pivotal lesson the day I made my final visit to his office. I expected to be praised during the visit, but what replayed in my mind was *"this is the advice you are leaving me with?"* I was deeply offended and convinced that this was all he knew to say to me.

However, now I am able to look back and see that He knew all along. He was not afraid to push through when I could not, or sit in the unknown with me until it became known. He would always tell me after every correction:

*"Pris, you know this stuff, you **see** the client, but you don't see yourself.*

"Be free, be flexible and avoid the why's swirling in your head. The why's cannot force the answer like you want them to. Be patient with yourself and you will learn to be patient with your client as well.

"Clients most of the time are a reflection of ourselves one way or another. This means, we have to do the work CONSTANTLY.

"Self-examination never stops, especially for those trained to self-examine

others."

Phew! This statement still brings me to my knees, as I unravel the intentionality it requires to see others clearly. By seeing, I am referring to the connection that is formed from a safe space with someone who understands your story and does not hold it against you.

To behold people as they are is an ongoing process. It reflects onto you how clearly you see yourself. How much more are you willing to confront yourself and your mistakes internally before you confront others?

Dr. M depicted grace onto me when I did not deserve it, he believed deeply in the process of my becoming when I didn't even know how to become or where to begin. As a result, I understood from a practical level the divine grace God bestows on us daily, even though it is often unrequited from our side, it is still unconditional and freely given.

My life verse is actually grounded on the basis of grace and at times it never made sense to me why this was my life verse, but along the way I realized… That is what the grace of God is. It is a gift that we do not deserve and to even provide the evidence as to why we deserve it, would still not measure up its greatness. It's one that cannot be purchased or deeply explained… Simple!

> *"But God's amazing grace has made me who I am! And his grace to me was not fruitless. In fact, I worked harder than all the rest, yet not in my own strength but God's, for his empowering grace, is poured out upon me."* 1 Corinthians 15:10 (TPT)

So, if you are reading this Dr. M aka best professor in my book, I appreciate you more than you know, and look at what I am doing now; I am being vulnerable.

I mentioned earlier that I would touch more on vulnerability in later chapters, so you will get to understand in more detail why it was such a struggle.

Now, if you are asking yourself, *'okay, now what? This was a great story, yay and praise be unto this "Dr. M" of yours, but how do **I** become a safe space? How* *do I do that, Priscilla?'*

Hang tight! I will provide more detail on what a safe space is from scholarly works later in the chapters, but for now, I will share with you from personal experience how you can learn to be a safe space.

First, you should invite yourself to *surrender* once again to the process of becoming daily. Remember the equation from the introduction?

$$\frac{\text{Courage}}{\text{Empathy + Vulnerability}} = \text{Becoming}$$

To do so properly and consistently takes courage. It means no longer allowing yourself to project, suppress or avoid unpleasant situations. Likewise, it requires you to operate from a space of empathy and vulnerability with yourself, which in turn, enables you to do so with others when they share their life experiences with you.

Secondly, gain a deep and personal understanding of the three principles from Chapter 2 titled *The Beginning of My Becoming*. Becoming means we go **through** the processes not move past them. Therefore, to create a deep and personal understanding of anything for that matter requires you to be intentional with your time.

Set aside time for reflection and do an activity that helps you reflect effectively whether that is walking, running, writing, singing, cooking, cleaning, etc. During this time, you learn to quiet your mind, analyze the situation before you, listen for answers, and sometimes arrive at a conclusion of what or where to go next. This time teaches you to be vulnerable with yourself, and ask those deep questions you tend to shy away from.

Similarly, it guides you to be gentle with yourself as you learn to alter your thinking patterns that you might have been unaware existed. I mentioned earlier that some behaviors are subconscious and conscious, but separating the two takes time and patience.

> *Author's Note: Notice that I said sometimes in the area of coming to a conclusion, and not always because some situations will require more time, the answer may not present itself right away. No matter the duration, the consistent message remains and that is, learn to surrender to the process.*

Last but not least, utilize these lessons **daily** in your personal and professional life. Learned behaviors do not improve overnight, but what does is the mental shift from "I do not need to change" to "I must change." Once this revelation becomes clear to you, it is your responsibility to monitor your behavior and make sure it reflects the new revelation. You cannot state you must change but still think or act in the same way you used to. This shift in behavior will take time and require grace on your part **daily.**

You see, becoming is not focused on reaching a certain destination or gaining a particular prize. Instead, it is the consistent march straight ahead to a space where change can occur over and over, and also a means for reaching onwards to be a better person.

If some relationships do not flow the way you intended as you begin to change and flourish in the new space; that is okay. You may realize that not all relationships will require your time and effort. Therefore, as you grow with these principles in mind, it is up to you to discern wisely who goes where. Additionally, the voices you want near and far as you begin to make choices that **finally** benefit you.

Now, when someone chooses to **openly** share with you who they are through their life story; that is a humbling experience and I believe that the foundation on which such an experience is built is ***vulnerability***. This word might as well have been a cuss word for me, but I threw it around to everyone else and demanded that they HAD to operate in it.

You know by now that I lived very opposing lives. I preached one thing but did another. Eventually, riding that wave of hypocrisy became impossible when I had to confront my inability to be vulnerable. This confrontation took place when it dawned on me during my check-ins with Dr. M highlighted in chapter 3, that I could see the client and their problems clearly. In turn, I would become frustrated with the client when they failed to see what I had deduced from their story.

As a counselor, I believed it was our job to highlight the problems people could not see in themselves and others. What I did not want to confront was the idea that I also had to learn to confront my own problems and let those in my inner circle do the same, before I did so with my clients. Most of all, I had to have the same patience I wanted people to have with me. All of this led me to internalize the mistakes I had made and that truly without a doubt... I was an imposter.

Often, as I shuffled to solve the mystery and understand people quickly I would interact with them from a place of *false empathy* and call it the real deal. I neglected any safe spaces they had formed and bulldozed my way through to make sure I became one of those safe spaces by force. Patience was not in my true vocabulary, but for others, it was a term I used dearly as I coerced them to tell me their story.

If you are thinking, *I will never let her get the best of me when we meet. My story is my story.* My dear friend rest assured that you have every right to think and feel as such because now, I realize the importance of vulnerability, empathy, and what it means to respect people's stories as well as safe spaces. I wish I would have had someone give me the same advice I am about to give you, but sometimes the lessons that are better learned in reverse, make a greater impact after the fact.

So, if you want to be an individual who operates in empathy and vulnerability authentically, here are a few things not to do.

1. *Never force or manipulate anyone into telling their story. Encourage, yes, but do so from a place of respect for their well-being.*
2. *Never rush to interject with your opinions, push aside, silence, or assume the role of chief editor. Instead, sit, listen and hold space.*

Although it is not my intent to sound repetitive, as mentioned earlier, I really struggled in my understanding of what empathy meant and how vulnerability played a role in it at all. Eventually, I had to get creative and remind myself of various ways to be empathetic as well as vulnerable.

This, in turn, helped me overcome my old behavior and thought patterns especially when the interactions became difficult to navigate. I knew manipulating the situation was not fair, but I would only remove myself from it when the need arose. So, not only did I learn these two terms properly, but I began to notice the unhealthy boundaries I had created for myself and how I used these unhealthy behaviors to cope or get out of them.

Now that I have shared with you some of my experiences with vulnerability, empathy, and holding space; I believe we have reached a good stopping point. In the next chapter, I will define these terms in more detail and how I came to learn of them but before we get into all of that, let's do a quick check-in.

1. How do you define vulnerability?

2. What has been your personal experience with this word?

3. How do you define empathy?

4. What has been your personal experience with this word?

5. How do you define holding space?

6. What has been your personal experience with this word?

4

The Enemy to Vulnerability

Dr. Brené Brown!

Say it loud and clear with me. If you've never heard of her, now's the time to put your bookmark down and go straight to Google.

Although I may never meet her face to face, I would like to thank her through these pages for normalizing that *it's okay to struggle with our emotions.*

Even when it became difficult to navigate vulnerability, I was inspired to seek after it time and time again through her research. Most of the time, it was easier to walk away from the confusion in my mind than to struggle restlessly trying to figure it out bit by bit.

On the contrary, in the back of my mind, I knew that right in the middle of my discomfort and struggle, lies breakthrough—that was *if I surrendered my ego.*

As an avid promoter of vulnerability now, back then it was all about keeping my dignity intact for the sake of staying "fresh" so to speak. I struggled with putting my emotions together to articulate what I was feeling, but for others, it seemed like a piece of cake.

Even when I was expressing difficult emotions, I wanted to *appeal* to people's strengths in the moment of their weaknesses and *pride* myself in doing so.

So, what is the "ego", you ask?

> "The ego **refuses** to be distressed by the provocations of reality, to let itself be compelled to suffer. It insists that it cannot be affected by the traumas of the external world; it shows, in fact, that such traumas are no more than occasions for it to **gain pleasure**."—Sigmund Freud (1917)[13]

The ego mentioned above is referred to as the self and mostly the *conscious sense*. It is also used in the Latin vernacular for the word "I." Recall the term projection introduced in Chapter One, this form of self-defense can be elicited *consciously* or *unconsciously*. In my experience, I used to do it consciously by drawing everything back to me from a positive light when it came time to blame shift and deal with the situation I knew I had caused negatively.

Sigmund Freud believed that there were two models pertaining to our physical structure as human beings, The Structural Model and The Topographical Model.

The Structural Model

The Structural Model is made up of three major systems: Id, Ego, and Superego. According to Freud, when these three systems work together they enable the individual to carry out structured and rewarding transactions within a person's environment.

From birth, humans innately seek out the desire to bring about self-satisfaction. However, these desires are sought out in different stages of our lives. An infant's primary motive is to always meet their needs, whether physical, mental, and environmental, as a means of survival. For example, an increase in hunger or thirst would prompt crying for the caregiver. Thus, the Id is very important early in life, because it ensures that the infant's needs are met.

This point in life is highly driven by the Id and acts on impulse without thought. Therefore, our actions are performed subconsciously instead of consciously. According to Sharf, "the means of operation for the id is the pleasure principle."[14]

As we progress in life, we learn to harness the Id's selfish impulses with the **ego's** help. We *relinquish* our fantasies to the *reality* of things and learn how to meet our needs *logically*. What we would have done *subconsciously* as an infant, we now learn to use another route *consciously* to have our needs met.

As we continue to mature in life, we begin to absorb parental values that in turn, shape our morals and influence our actions. These moral codes that we form for ourselves are a result of the **superego**. Whereas the Id and Ego are aspects of the individual, this part of our personality is highly influential because it incorporates all the others in its processing.[15]

The superego is the side of our personality that houses all of our integrated moral standards and ideals that we acquire from parents and society; clearly speaking, it is our sense of right and wrong. According to Freud, the superego begins to emerge at around the age of five.

I mentioned above how well these three systems work when they are in sync. However, when you are struggling to deal with the reality of any negative experience, whether the loss of a friend or a job, the ego will find ways to cope without falling back into id behavior.

Repression, denial, and projection are just some of the defense mechanisms you may begin to form due to that adversity. Also, any rejection, sexual, physical, and verbal abuse that occurs or has occurred in your life may influence your inconsistent use of these defense mechanisms to keep your ego from deteriorating.

Insight within the *unconscious* is the first step of change in regards to unhealthy functioning, and in this phase, you are capable of realizing your true self. Most of this change is aided through safe spaces and safe voices that come through therapy sessions, spiritual mentorship, support from loved ones, local community havens, and more.

"Self-understanding is achieved through analysis of childhood experiences that are reconstructed, interpreted, and analyzed."[16]

These assessments allow the individual to realize what his or her motives were unconscious, and in turn, deal with the real issue at hand consciously.

The Topographical Model

The Topographical Model consists of the conscious, preconscious, and unconscious mind. Sounds confusing, right?

I know it was during graduate school when this was being explained, I was that person who had to SA-UNN-D (sound) it out, to understand it.

Now, the conscious mind consists of everything that we are aware of. This is the piece of our mental processing that we use to think and talk about rationally. The preconscious mind, however, is part of the conscious mind but also includes our memory. These memories are not conscious, but we can call them to our conscious awareness at any time.

On the other hand, the unconscious mind stores our feelings, thoughts, urges, and memories that are outside of our conscious awareness. The contents of our unconscious can be either pleasant or unpleasant, such as feelings of pain, anxiety, or conflict.

According to Freud, even though we are unaware, the unconscious influences our behaviors and experiences. Below, you will find The Topographical Model Diagram that consists of the three structural systems as well for a more visual understanding; give it up for my spatial(visual) learners, I got you!

THE ENEMY TO VULNERABILITY

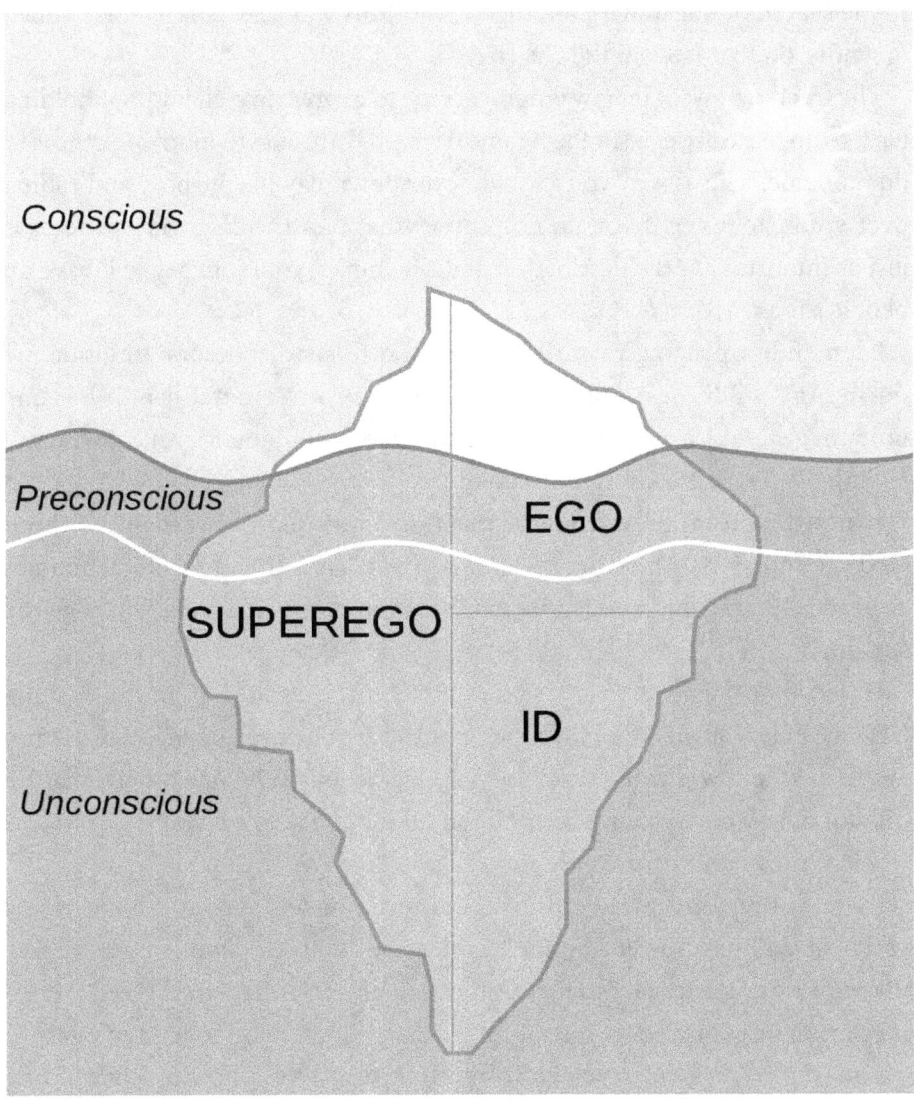

It's clear that the distance I have traveled towards becoming a better person has been fueled by the labor of researchers before my time. Gaining insight regarding the levels of my mind through rued and many other researchers helped me rest in the normalcy that the struggle to sort out our emotions is a never-ending journey.

Likewise, Dr. Brené Brown and the revelation of what vulnerability meant in the search of our understanding of emotions was a reckoning. Stay tuned for more on that later in the chapter.

The freedom I walk in now empowers me to express myself without holding back to appease my ego. In that frame of mind, I am able to motivate others to do the same. This is why you should never downplay the purpose and calling over your life. Even if you do not know what it is, the discovery process is just as important as the destination and the impact your journey will have on people's lives.

I remember praying relentlessly for God to send someone to guide me during my wilderness season especially when my mental health became unmanageable. I would drive home from work sobbing for an answer and feeling like I was watching life pass me by.

I knew that if I moved from the position I was in professionally, without God's permission or blessing it would be from a posture of rebellion and not of peace. Having that awareness made it even more difficult to manage the season.

I cried almost daily in the presence of the Lord questioning Him and asking Him why He was the most sovereign God yet not answering me. Was He not aware of what I was going through? Was He too busy blessing others, that He did not have time to glance over His shoulder and see my pain?

'What meaneth this,' I would inquire over and over again?

I would pray and plead using all sorts of Shakespeare and King James vernacular I knew to get a better "connection" with God while I was yelling through my pain towards Him. Albeit my efforts, I never received a deep revelation or explanation, but simply heard the word *wait* over and over.

Looking back, God revealed to me that when we find ourselves going through painful trials and tribulations, we tend to perceive them as *personal attacks* or shortcomings from Him. This assumption that He is either angry with you or does not love you is sometimes fueled by the emotions that one feels over time as a result of waiting with no clear direction or answer.

These periods of discomfort are pit-stops and opportunities for growth along the way and God uses them to add to your story. You may be the instrument God uses to change a multitude of people. It may feel painful and

THE ENEMY TO VULNERABILITY

unfair, but the outcome is larger than what you see in front of you.

5

And So I Waited

Waiting around for something that is logically and practically impossible may seem silly to you and onlookers, but to me, that is the beauty of faith.

When my focus shifted away from what I saw in front of me, and beyond what God had promised me, I began to comprehend what faith was in the eyes of God.

If we are to please God, we first have to *know* and *believe* that he exists. It's one thing to know, but to believe is another (further explanation on this later). Our belief in Him is the reason we chose to follow Him and because of that choice, everything we do strives to be pleasing unto Him.

Love and Pride

Love does not say it cares about someone, yet every day, it's speaking down on them. Love does not act against its meaning. If it was to do so, we would call that pride. Pride likes to hide within its own meaning. It presents itself as blameless in our sights but at the same time it is the first to throw blame behind the curtains.

Pride is an *ego* seeker but presents itself to the public eye as the *superego* of self. It claims to work from the unconscious realm, forgetting what was said and done. Yet, it was clearly *present* and *conscious* throughout the whole "act."

Your decision to follow God should be blameless and without fault. As a matter of fact, God wants you to come to His throne room as bold as you are because from that posture, He is able to receive you blamelessly and without fault.

> *"Let us then approach God's throne of grace with **confidence**, so that we may **receive** mercy and find grace to help us in our time of need"* Hebrews 4:16 (NIV).

When we approach life in this manner, we operate from a posture of faith that we never knew we had access to because of our ***unbelief!***

> *"Without faith living within us, it would be impossible to please God.[e] For we come to God in faith **knowing** that he is real and that he **rewards** the faith of those who passionately seek him"* Hebrews 11:6 (TPT).

As a young girl, I knew that I was created for greatness, and the emotions and thoughts I faced then and still now, do not define or rule out what God is going to do.

You may be wondering what it is that God has promised you. If so, go back to Him **boldly** and ask.

He is able, ready, and willing to provide you with an answer! However, do not limit Him, due to your lack of understanding, regarding how that answer will come. Instead, surrender to the process, hold firm to the promise within and *wait for Him.*

Waiting does not diminish our faith, instead, it increases it beyond our hopes and dreams because we ***learn how*** to wait properly. I learned during my season of waiting that God does not attend to groaners and whiners. Yes, he wants us to cry out to him and still loves us no matter what we do.

Although how we approach and wait for Him does matter, sometimes we think it's God who delays. However, most of the time, dare I say 99% of the time, it is us because of our attitude in the waiting. God is the ultimate promise keeper. Better yet the ultimate covenant keeper. He keeps both His and our side of the deal whether we depart from it completely or just a little while; He is still there waiting.

Let me ask you, have you ever witnessed someone groaning and whining for something that they had every right to but their attitude was terrible?

By that, I mean that they had every right to ask for what they later received, but the manner in which they did so was not pleasing but rather harsh and rude. Was it off-putting to you or tolerable?

When I came to God in such a way, I left feeling more guilt than freedom. Did He not see how well I was waiting? I deserved to be served my due diligence. Uh-oh, yeah, that's right! I realized I was playing in the wrong territory. My mother reminded me strongly one day that God is not a man that we can **manipulate** through our cries and wants. He is the one who judges and sees clearly the hearts of men and women.

We may see stature and success but God sees otherwise. When Samuel was sent by God to go anoint the next king of Israel, Samuel judged immediately by his first look and thought his task was done; he was immediately warned by God that:

> "**Looks aren't everything**. Don't be impressed with his looks and stature. I've already eliminated him. **God judges persons differently** than humans do. Men and women look at the face; God looks into the **heart**"
> 1 Samuel 16:7 (MSG).

Through my fits of rage and resentment towards God as well as His people, I *rushed* to succeed in everything I "thought I knew" during and even after my graduate studies. I did not study fully for my state licensure exam because I believed that I was equipped with the full knowledge and if not God would give it to me, he owed me that. Right? I mean, look how good I was and had become vulnerable with myself and others. I was rocking this thing.

No matter what I made it look like or how calmly I behaved towards others to show God, He knew my heart was not ready at all but oh, I thought it was! I had plenty of receipts and arguments to prove my point, yet my perception of justice was not His. Remember that piece about pride and ego; that was the territory I was living in. Womp, womp, womp...

God's sovereignty will remain whether he chooses to prove or give you a thing. As a matter of fact, He does not have to prove or give you anything! Yet even in His sovereignty, He remains the same and chooses to commune with us daily no matter what. Thus, you and I must be careful to not *grieve* the spirit of God.

> *"Watch the way you talk. Let nothing foul or dirty come out of your mouth. Say only what helps, each word a gift. Don't grieve God. Don't **break his heart**. His Holy Spirit, **moving** and **breathing** in you, is the most **intimate** part of your life, making you **fit** for himself. Don't take such a gift for granted. Make a clean break with all cutting, backbiting, profane talk. Be gentle with one another, sensitive. Forgive one another as quickly and thoroughly as God in Christ forgave you"* Ephesians 4:29-32 (MSG).

Now, as you wait you want to do so with a good attitude but this does not reduce the frustration or doubts that may occur along the way. Fixing your eyes on the promise of God builds a spiritual reservoir in you to access in times of hopelessness.

> *"There's more to come: We continue to shout our praise even when we're hemmed in with troubles, because we know how troubles can develop passionate patience in us, and how that patience, in turn, forges the tempered steel of virtue, keeping us alert for whatever God will do next"* Romans 5:3 (MSG).

Every time you make a *conscious effort* to focus beyond what you see physically, you invite God to complete that GOOD work in you, as you sit, surrender, and wait *patiently* with hope. For hope does NOT disappoint.

Let me share with you the *main* verse that guided me through the season of drought in my life and quenched the spiritual thirst within. From it, I was able to see why faith and hope worked in tandem as vital weapons in the hands of those seated and waiting in the wilderness for God.

> *"Now faith **brings our hopes into reality** and **becomes the foundation needed to acquire the things we long for**. It is **all the evidence** required to prove what is **still** unseen. This testimony of faith is what previous generations were commended for. Faith **empowers us** to see that the universe was created and beautifully coordinated by the power of God's words! He **spoke** and the **invisible realm gave birth to all that is seen**"* Hebrews 11:1-3 (TPT).

As this verse began to minister to me daily, my mind and emotions began to shift towards that which He promised me. Whether I was feeling up or down, I kept pushing through the discomfort and most of all speaking into the unseen that which I believed I would see through the faithfulness of God. It's not just enough to believe it, you have to proclaim it daily until it becomes ingrained in your heart.

Even writing this book was a process of telling myself verbally that I was a good writer and that God had equipped me with everything I needed to succeed. I just needed to channel it through Him and not in my strength alone!

Phillip Yancey, another incredible author describes faith as, *"believing in advance what will only make sense in reverse."* This idea also launched me into realms of freedom I never knew I had access to or existed. God was okay with me not understanding the whole process. As a matter of fact, He had already given me permission to not make sense of it all!

The nitty-gritty details of how everything would work itself out for GOOD was His responsibility, not mine. Oh, what relief came to my mind, heart, and soul when I anchored myself in that truth! On the contrary, this was not always easy, but I formed a habit of checking into all three (mind, heart & soul) when I noticed I was striving to make things happen in my own strength.

I learned to be assertive when it came to my thoughts and emotions; inviting myself daily to navigate those spaces that brought up confusion, unrest, or fear.

Whatever the emotion or thought was, I knew that addressing it was where the story began to form itself. What people, society, and or the enemy meant for evil, God began to turn it around for good.

Personally, I wish I had received the guidance I am sharing with you now, but looking back God had bigger plans not just for me. Although I had to navigate the wilderness alone, the journey created a story that God is now using to reveal to many that feel this way just how much He cares and understands them. I needed to live or better yet, wait for God to finish the good work in me that would be used to release freedom to many.

At the moment it may not feel pleasant and it may feel like you have been camped in the "wilderness" for way too long, but rest assured it all comes together to form a message of hope.

One that will inspire someone else who is also soul searching for that place they know they are called to but do not know where or how to get there. Allow me to share with you, one of the many bible verses that kept me going during my times of despair, loneliness, and etc.

> "Meanwhile, the moment we get tired **in the waiting**, God's Spirit is right **alongside** helping us along. If we don't know how or what to pray, it doesn't matter. He does our praying in and for us, making prayer out of our wordless sighs, our aching groans. He knows us far better than we know ourselves, knows our **pregnant condition**, and keeps us present before God. That's why we can be so sure that **every detail** in our lives of love for God **is worked** into something good" Romans 8:26-28 (MSG).

This verse affirms the waiting process, period! Now, pause, and let's insert here: Thank God! Because at some point I had begun to believe that I was the only one God was making "wait." We thank God for freedom.

Now, moving on, this verse also affirms the emotions we tend to neglect or *suppress* because they "sound crazy", and assures us that there is **one** who understands what we are feeling without us even speaking a word. How awesome is that?

For those that may be lost in translation, what I mean here is that God uses all of the unpleasant things we walk through to make sure the end result turns out good for us. That is, His main focus is that while you are waiting, you aren't waiting idly but being grown for something good. The destination has to be prepared for you, and you for it.

You may say, 'Priscilla, are you saying that God causes bad things to happen in our lives to make up for Himself or make Himself look good?'

No, I am definitely not. I am saying that he uses those things **bad or good** (in this case we are focusing on the not-so-good). to grow us internally while at the same time forming something good for us to encounter along the way.

One of my pastors during my years at university said it this way, *"God does not have to be the author of something, to be the LORD of it."*

In sum, God is sovereign and in His sovereignty, he is able to turn a mess around that we probably got ourselves into. If that is the case, He could easily say that is your fault, now you fix it. Instead, being the good God that He always is, He takes on the mistake like it was His and turns it around for our benefit.

Likewise, even if we did not cause the mess and are in it, he is still capable of turning it around. So if you are currently in a season of waiting and you feel as if God is distant, be encouraged. Romans 8:26-28 reminds us that God is *preparing* a place for you, so that when you get there, you can finally let go of your luggage, take a deep breath and say, I have arrived.

You can confidently declare, with peace in your heart, that this is it. This is where I am supposed to be, the place where God has *called* me… The place, where purpose and destiny meet.

6

The Difficulty in Vulnerability

In the final stretch of my second year of my Master's program, one of the assignments required us to begin exploring what vulnerability meant to us. I remember that day clearly, as I sat in my room wondering why I was pursuing this degree. I drew a blank as I stared at the computer screen waiting for something magical to happen and oh, it did.

All of these exercises were necessary for our training as future clinicians who would be tasked with the responsibility of being a safe space for many. Dr. M made it clear that it was unfair to ask someone to do something you wouldn't be willing to do. Thus, exploring vulnerability for ourselves was highly expected throughout the program.

I also believe this was the heart posture that God wanted to see that. The one I was referring to in the previous chapter one; of humility and grace. I did not know how the help would come and I did not care what it looked like. All I know is that I was in desperate need of it. Aside from the state licensing exam and proving myself to everyone, this was more important. I could not lie my way through this as I had before many times, no. N, this time it had to be genuine for my future depended on it.

Our coursework included student-to-student counseling, student-to-teacher counseling, group counseling as a class, and personal journal assignments. Most of these courses were also videotaped and evaluated as a class. How awkward, right?

This was my least favorite part since most of my colleagues were expected to properly critique my habits. Eventually, a classmate noticed how I would avoid certain questions during the tape evaluation.

Immediately, I became nervous and defensive. My tricks and tactics were no longer hidden, and boom. Anxiety exploded in my heart as I did not want to be seen. Nevertheless, this became the turning point for me.

My professor along with the whole class confronted me for my inability to be vulnerable.

Remember those sections about Imposter Syndrome and my regular check-ins with my professor? You can imagine how tired I was after long nights of counseling, which forced me to be vulnerable and then having to face a tape evaluation the very next day to defend my false vulnerability as a pass in the class.

Now, I am thankful for every lesson along the way. And to all that still struggle like me with vulnerability, there is no one-stop destination. Instead, we evolve along the way in our ability to be vulnerable people.

Rational Emotive Behavioral Therapy

During the duration of my masters, Rational Emotive Behavioral Therapy (REBT) was my theory of choice and still is today. REBT was coined by Dr. Albert Ellis who believed that the majority of our irrational behaviors and emotions were the consequences of our irrational beliefs (thought) patterns.

As my theory of choice, REBT required me as the counselor to be direct and assertive in order to lead my client towards a moment of confrontation also known as *disputing* the client's irrational thinking according to Dr. Ellis's A-B-C- model.

Ellis's theory is arranged around three different views: social, biological, and philosophical. All of these viewpoints tie into his A-B-C model mentioned above that he formed to understand personality and effectively change the client's irrational beliefs of themselves or the events that occurred in their life.

The philosophical perspectives of this theory include hedonism, humanism, and rationality. Hedonism refers to the human nature of seeking out pleasure to avoid momentary pain and although Ellis believed this was inherent in us all, he encouraged the pursuit of long-term pleasure instead.

When we seek out momentary pleasures to avoid or suppress mental and emotional pain, our behavior turns maladaptive, meaning it inhibits the proper *adjustment to new situations or environments.* For example, an individual can start to constantly use drugs or alcohol to avoid school or work due to a new move or family conflict.

Through the eyes of humanism, humans are viewed as, *"holistic, goal-directed organisms who are important because they are alive."*[17] Additionally, humans should have **unconditional self-acceptance** for themselves and **accept** that they make mistakes but remain worthy *regardless* of what happens in life.

Therefore, being rational can help an individual lead a successful life and achieve their goals. Using proper judgment, *flexibility*, and using resourceful techniques helps an individual re-examine teachings in life that he or she may have just accepted as a rule of thumb without question.

Perception vs. Reality

Remember when I believed that everyone needed rescuing? And also when I believed every client I would see in the future would be the same or at least have the same story? Surrendering to the process of becoming required an extensive phase of re-examining the teachings I had imagined and accepted as truth.

My Intro into Perception and Cognition professor during my undergraduate studies always reminded us of the fact that *"Perception is not always reality."* What I perceive to be my reality and my truth is not always the same as the other person. Therefore, when we encounter new people and take in their stories, we have to cognitively remember to place our perceptions of their reality aside.

For example, the interview with Prince Harry, Meghan Markle, and Oprah was a defining moment in history as to why we as the public eye should never view someone's story through our lenses only or through what the tabloids or anyone else have to say.

During the interview, Meghan made a statement that "when the perception and the reality are two very different things and you're being judged on the perception but you're living the reality of it, there's a complete misalignment."

She went on to address how difficult it was to be her authentic self when she was constantly met with demands and expectations that she didn't even know how to meet. In addition to that, the more she tried to understand and explain herself, the more she was put off.

As she sat there explaining the constant defeat between the struggle to adjust, please, and be free, I felt her pain deeply because I also knew that struggle before. Once I began to practice unconditional self-acceptance through the act of surrender and allowing myself to be seen and be seen as who I was not what the world thought, changes began to happen.

To understand someone's entire story, we should strive to function from an intrinsic space of empathy. However, if we continue rushing to finish first while forcing incorrect pieces into the puzzle calling it complete, we will miss out on reality.

As we begin to surrender the maladaptive beliefs we once held for ourselves, and the world to gain a new understanding; exemplifying our new beliefs authentically becomes easier.

For example, when Prince Harry commented, *"I was trapped but I didn't know I was trapped."* He said meeting Meghan was what allowed him to *"see a way out."*

Ellis described the biological factors of humans as having the ability or in other words, the choice to choose how to react to specific events in our lives. He believed that comprehending the philosophical aspect of re-examining our values and teachings in life acted as a catalyst to effectively change our social and behavioral factors.

Activating Events

According to Sharf, humans *"react to events in certain patterns, regardless of environmental factors that may affect events, by damning themselves and others..."*[18] Social factors also come into effect since they directly influence *vulnerability* to a disturbance.

Was my theory of choice a way to escape and justify my behavior towards others? Yes, yes it was.

I can say it confidently now, but back then I wouldn't have dared. What acted as a means of escape only revealed the deep and painful truth that I had been functioning in irrational thinking for so long and that I perceived it as normal. Likewise, my perception of reality towards others was that they were irrational. Wow! Talk about a TASTE of your own medicine.

The nature of humans in this sense is that we each have factors in our lives that form our belief system and consequently cause an emotional or behavioral response. The A-B-C model perfectly illustrates and explains how we are driven to react to specific events, good or bad, as well as how this builds our perspective throughout life. Sharf provides a good example of the model with the following:

> "Individuals have goals that may be supported or thwarted by **activating events** (As). They then react, consciously or unconsciously, with their **belief system** (B), by which they respond to the activating event with something such as, "This is nice." They also experience the **emotional or behavioral consequence** (C) of the activating event."[19]

Ellis also elaborates on rational beliefs and explores how they drive us to react after a specific situation pleasant or unpleasant. In this case, the more pleasant a situation is, the more it goes *unnoticed*.

When our expectations are not met or when we stumble upon a situation that is unfamiliar to us, we strive to make sense of it as creatures of habit. As a result, our minds go into a state of frenzy, as we search for the right solution amid our adversity.

However, most of the time, that solution or belief system is irrational and is guided by emotion. Once this belief system is set in motion, our behaviors begin to reflect it towards ourselves and others.

For example, if you saw pictures of your friends online somewhere having a good time and you were not invited, you may wonder why they did not invite you. Do they not like me anymore? As those thoughts swirl in your mind, a belief system is formed that what you have seen and the resulting feelings are true; no one can convince you otherwise.

Consequently, your behavior begins to reflect this belief you hold of your friends through passive-aggressive behavior. For example, you begin avoiding them, acting out with other people you have chosen to befriend, etc.

In sum, disturbances occur when individuals *wish* for something to occur *their* way, and it fails to. As described by Sharf, *"when the activating event is unpleasant, many different beliefs and consequences can result."*[20] This causes a healthy emotional and behavioral response such as the determination to do better and learn from mistakes or an unhealthy response like *stagnation or lack of confidence* in self. Overall, stunting any intrinsic motivation towards growth.

The consequences to a belief system are endless but simply said, this theory teaches us to slow down and process the events in our lives that most likely were 100% true, and every feeling or thought we held of them was valid. However, moving forward we can learn to assess situations before we rush to a conclusion that alters our belief patterns towards others and most of all towards ourselves.

That being said, these courses were really difficult internally but externally, I coasted through. Remember I was the master at hiding my feelings and instead focusing on others. My thought patterns were really skewed and it wasn't until I quit fighting myself that I realized the amount of self-work I had to do.

Environmental Impact

Can you recall the environments or spaces of confusion, unknowns, and despair? Weren't those the spaces I mentioned we needed to lean into and deal with our hesitancies with vulnerability? Well, I was definitely going through those spaces all at once but surely the wilderness season wasn't going to last this long; so I thought.

Ellis was an advocate of the idea that environmental impact determined the individual's view on life, themselves, and others. This revolved around the vulnerability to disturbance as discussed earlier, and if not properly addressed could lead to unhealthy functioning, which was where I was heading.

During this phase of clinicals, we were trying to keep ourselves afloat as we managed clinic hours outside of school, assignments, and personal lives. If you stopped one of us now randomly and asked what phrase we heard the most during clinicals, we would say: "practice self-care." This phrase was simple to acknowledge audibly, but actually doing it was a challenge for me in addition to the vulnerability and REBT work.

Simply doing an activity you enjoyed like getting a massage, going to see a movie or anything that allowed your mind to relax without clouding your judgment was considered self-care. From this lens, it was imperative to be of sober mind in order to fully be present with both yourself and the client.

To maintain my sanity, I mastered the art of easily speeding my way through mock clinical sessions to avoid getting too vulnerable. However, that always backfired when it was time to assess my tapes as you read previously. My professor relentlessly confronted my hesitations in displaying or receiving emotions and reminded me that locking myself in my head would not sustain me.

On the other hand, my family was praising me for succeeding in my studies, but little did they know the struggle it was to maintain their praise and my falsehood. I pondered on this role many times and felt guilty for not sharing with them how hard it was to maintain their praises. I knew deep down that they would be accepting of me whether I succeeded or not but I wasn't able to face my vulnerability nor did I have the courage or empathy in myself to sit through a discussion like that.

As I studied my theory of choice thoroughly, it occurred to me while writing this book why REBT deeply resonated with me. It wasn't because of the irrational dispute and directiveness of the clinician. However, it was this role that the environment played described by Ellis here:

Social factors according to REBT theory are vital in determining whether individuals view themselves as worthy or not. He or she will only regard themselves highly when they see others doing so. For example, if parents hold their child to high standards such as praising them for every accomplishment; the child will feel a sense of self-esteem and positive regard for themselves and others.

However, all of that began to change after my divine encounter with Dr. Brown's Ted Talk on the *Power of Vulnerability*. I felt connected to her personality immediately. As a helping professional who championed this phrase and used it more in one day than most people, I despised it personally in many ways, as she did too.

She mentions in the video how leaning into the discomfort is a commonly used phrase in most social sciences. Just like me, she wanted to knock discomfort upside the head, move it aside and get all the good grades instead.

This was the perfect description of who I was and how I navigated clinicals as well as my whole life honestly. I finally felt seen by someone whom I did not know. She explained clearly what I could not when I was tasked with explaining why it was so difficult to embrace vulnerability to the professor.

I never shared this phase with anyone else during my studies or counseling sessions and for all they knew, I was an easy-going person who liked to be direct in her sessions until the day I was confronted by my peers.

If anyone from my cohort is reading this, I am still that same easy-going and direct person but now, I appreciate what it means to be vulnerable and I have acquired a bit more patience than I had then.

Also, I apologize for being so defensive that day. I was trying to move past the opportunity of growth instead of working my way through it with people who saw what I was capable of becoming.

7

The Change I Needed

Who has God used to change your life so drastically that no one can tell you otherwise? When you reflect on how far you have come, this person always pops up in your testimony of grace. For me, it was none other than Dr. Brené Brown as mentioned previously.

God is always working behind the scenes for our good and I can recall the moment where I gained a deeper revelation of what that was. As I sat in my room debating my worth, my degree, and if I was ill well equipped for a career in counseling, God was up to something bigger than I could imagine.

Remember when I mentioned that He goes before us to prepare a place for our good? And that in all things, not just some, He always uses it for our good because He is good? Well, there was a moment I didn't understand how my feelings of despair and loneliness could yield any good.

I wondered if God even cared an ounce about my internal pain and struggle to find out who I am. Thankfully, God used Dr. Brown to change my life drastically that night and forevermore.

One that particular night, I was in such a space of despair and after stumbling on her YouTube video, it became an escape into the depths of my mind.

Truthfully, I did not want to disclose the reasons for my struggle with vulnerability. I was not keen on the idea of having to disclose my weakness and on the other hand, find an author who supported or embraced it as a strength. It was my pride and ego all over again, and goodness, was I swimming in it. I was fuming with arguments to support my claims that vulnerability was for sissies, literally. I viewed it as the one thing that could tear down the armor that you had righteously built to protect yourself from all evil.

I prided myself in the so-called "armor of God" that I carried. To me, vulnerability was a weapon that could harm you if not used correctly. Thus, the armor. I believed that people used special methods and tactics in the name of vulnerability as a way to draw out the deep things in you. They did this not only to understand you but to also know your weak points and gain insight on where to attack most.

I equated vulnerability with manipulation because that was something I had unfortunately dealt with my whole life. My experience as a young girl in Kenya and the numerous voices taught me that the voices of others were sent to guide me on what career path or choice to take. Thus, as I entered middle school and high school it became clear that pleasing was the path to take to avoid disappointing my parent's name.

My father is a very well renowned minister of the Gospel who has preached on many platforms that most people like you and I would be privileged to. Carrying his name was not something to take lightly, but I chose to carry it like a burden instead of a trophy.

Throughout my childhood and adulthood, this not only became a tug of war but an identity crisis that led me into depression, which I will go into detail later. For now, just know that vulnerability had not *yet* yielded any good fruit in my life back then. As a matter of fact, it only lessened the fruit I had or wanted to give.

Picture the secret garden movie or any garden that was once beautiful but now looks dingy and dry; this was my heart. Taps were leaking, birds weren't chirping as they used to, the sun barely shined and if it did, it was for a mere moment. On the outside, the carrier of the garden seemed perfectly fine, but inside it had been long since anyone had seen or tended to the garden. However, a ray of sunshine began to peek through the clouds revealing a source of hope. Not all was lost as it seemed.

As I listened to Dr. Brown explain her truth and substantiate her battle with being a vulnerability researcher, the data began to make sense to me. All along, Dr. Brené Brown was sent to research people like me and through that, she began to understand herself. What seemed impossible or uncomfortable to her was the place and space she chose to lean into to receive breakthroughs.

Immediately, an immeasurable wave of revelation began to fill my heart and mind. God was speaking to me and it was the clearest I had ever heard Him. Before I move on, let me address or better yet call out this conflict many of us in Christendom go through but refuse to claim because of the shame or guilt we may feel among our peers.

The battle to second ourselves when we hear the voice of God is real but it is barely addressed. It is often slapped and covered with numerous scriptures shaming us about why we should be privileged to speak and hear from God.

Although those scriptures speak the truth and do provide revelation to the seeker, the inability to sit in someone's pain with them as they desperately seek out a solution to this never-ending struggle is the problem with the church.

Jokes aside, the mental struggle to connect with God and hear His voice was real y'all. *I had to insert some Texan slang there for my Texans.* The consequence of my inability to connect and be vulnerable with people also leaked into my spiritual life. I would read the Word of God, sing, even lead worship at church, but inside I was dead. I would watch others connect with God and cry out to Him in full support of what they were seeking; all while internally wishing I could seek it too.

I wrestled with my intellect and spirit in my attempt to understand this supreme God, the Maker of heaven and earth. I did not believe that He had anything worthwhile to say to me and unbelievably, I became comfortable with having prophets speak on His behalf to me. They had a better relationship with God. Why not me?

This was not to say the ministry of prophecy was not enough or worthwhile, in fact, it was necessary for birthing who I am today. I used ministry as an altar to praise my God when in fact, I needed to be the true sacrifice before Him so that He could speak to me directly.

I was thankful for the prophets in my life, but even they could not usher me into the presence of God. It was my decision to do so. Thus, I learned to throw away every third voice, and commune with God by myself so as to learn His voice in my life.

Lastly, I was thankful for my parents who cultivated a life of prayer and intimacy with God to the extent that outside voices were rarely needed. This is not to say that advice did not come, but it meant that it was not all our strength leaned on. I began to understand that God was truly the source of everything I needed, even if a timely word came my way.

As I grew in my knowledge of God and His character, it dawned on me that we tend to complicate Him. This complication arises when we knowingly and unknowingly **spiritually bypass** ourselves or others who wrestle with understanding the character of God. This battle is not something an individual may have intended to walk through but their life circumstances might have led them there.

Spiritual Bypassing

John Welwood was the first to coin the term spiritual bypassing in 1984 and defined it as an easy ticket out for individuals who find it difficult to navigate their way through the developmental stages of life. Over time, it became apparent to Welwood that people will suppress their personal needs and identity with their spiritual practices.

As mentioned by Picciotto, Gabriela, Fox, & Neto, heavily reading books on spirituality, engaging in spiritual practices, visiting spiritual leaders, attending spiritual retreats, or joining spiritual communities without directly addressing or nurturing one's psychological needs are some of the behaviors of spiritual bypassers.[21]

The idea is rooted in the belief that one's spiritual work may one day deliver them from their psychological suffering. However, ignoring the psychological work increases the risk of stunted emotional development and could lead to greater psychological suffering.

> *"Masters identified the main symptoms of spiritual bypass as repression and emotional alienation, exaggerated detachment, overemphasis on the positive, blind compassion or excessive tolerance, minimization or denial of the shadow side of one's personality, overconfidence about self-awakening, the notion that everything is an illusion including suffering, and disregarding the personal or mundane."*[22]

I would like to tie in scripture here to prove to you that Jesus also made it clear that we would still go through trials and tribulations, but that He would overcome them all (John 16:33). In the midst of your suffering, there is hope for a new morning and in the waiting season, a voice that understands your pain.

In seasons of suffering, you and I have a High Priest who mediates on our behalf (Hebrews 4:14-16). This is to say, that we should not be *quick* to bypass suffering as the spiritual. Jesus acknowledged our pain and made it clear that it would in fact happen and through that, He said that we should take hold of Him for He had overcome the world.

He could have easily said I will take away all the pain so do not be afraid, but instead, He proclaimed His sovereignty over that which would be the cause of our pain.

> *"I have told you these things, so that **in Me** you may have peace. In this world, **you will** have trouble. But take heart! I have overcome the world."*
> John 16:33

To conclude, what are some statements you have used to spiritually bypass your own emotions or someone else's? What are some insights you have gained?

My oh my, have we come far along this journey. I look forward to seeing you on the other side. Here's to moving through our pain, not past it as we continue to surrender to the process of becoming.

8

The Change I Believe In

Can you recall the social factors discussed in Ellis's REBT theory and how individuals learn to practice *unconditional* self-acceptance once they re-examine their irrational thinking in order to gain a new perspective?

Ellis believed that once we accept ourselves authentically without the influence of others, we could begin to form beliefs that we deeply align with and not just those we have been taught to accept as truth.

Now, the last two final steps of this theory reflect what we, as the church, should work on helping individuals work through their pain, not move past it, as I mentioned in the previous chapter.

Empathy has no script. It's simply holding space for those hurting. However, sometimes the pressure to *move past* someone else's pain is more appealing than sitting with them in that space of discomfort. Even if a solution does not arise at the moment, we must not rush to find one ourselves.

Perhaps that is what God intends for us to do—sit with them. Is that not enough? Why do we feel such a burden to "fix" things or people? Yes, the altruistic nature is good but is the outcome good? And what does it benefit? Rushing to find scripture for reference and say a quick prayer may be appropriate at times, but not *all* the time.

REBT's A-B-C model incorporates two additional steps to complete the cycle of change within the individual and that is **step D:** disputing the belief that leads to **step E:** effective change within.

Step D is the step we tend to rush through as Christians in the church because we want to see immediate change especially when it revolves around mental health. It's as if this struggle is not one we, as the church, should "delight" in for long but move past it.

When I use the word delight here, I am referring to the idea of focusing or spending time on it. We should be fighting for their freedom with every chapter, book, retreat, and song we have.

Now, please do not misinterpret my heart here because I do believe all of these things add to the individual's deliverance process. I strongly believe that worship does change the atmosphere. It shifts our mind to focus on who is great around us, and not on what is great in front of us or within us.

Declaring the Scriptures play a vital role to edify people's minds, will, and emotions, but so does being a sounding board to the individual.

Let's not forget, that is who God is to us. He is not just a Father who redeems, protects, corrects, delivers, heals and so much more. He is the one who listens quietly as we disclose the contents of our hearts. Furthermore, He chooses to listen as if it is the first time even though He already knows what we need before we even ask (Matthew 6:8).

He is so simple in His ways that man cannot fathom it and as creatures of habit, we tend to force understanding upon ourselves as if the *Ultimate Giver of wisdom* is not enough for us.

1 Corinthians challenges this innate response within us to shun the revelations of God when they seem foolish to our understanding and correct us.

> *"But the natural [unbelieving] man does not accept the things [the teachings and revelations] of the Spirit of God, for they are foolishness [absurd and illogical] to him; and he is incapable of understanding them, because they are spiritually discerned and appreciated, [and he is unqualified to judge spiritual matters]"* 1 Corinthians 2:14 (AMP).

As smooth as butter, clearer than any crystal waters, I heard the voice of God begin to speak to my soul (mind, will, and emotions). As Dr. Brown's video regarding the power vulnerability played in the background, this verse came to life, and instantly the strenuous, ongoing war in my soul depleted of itself.

I listened *clearly* without a shift or distraction in my mind for the first time, as God sifted through the issues I had been struggling with one by one. I got a revelation on why He used and would continue to use those struggles to complete His good work in me.

In tandem, as Dr. Brown confidently articulated her personal struggles and what led her to do this research, God was also confidently speaking to me regarding *why* He called me to be a counselor.

I also began to understand *why* I dove headfirst when the opportunity to be holding space for someone arose and why the struggle to be vulnerable was so persistent in my life.

As I *surrendered* to this new season that God was calling me to move through, flourish in, and ultimately become a new creation in His eyes, I learned to commit to memory that all of my shortcomings both past, present or future were being *turned around in good faith for my good.*

Most importantly, God **continued** to work with me on discerning His voice among the rest, especially. E, in the wilderness season where the temptation to create my own oasis and find retreat in other things was becoming quite strong. I knew I had free will, and I knew that at any moment I could make a call, drive or fly somewhere else to escape this calling.

However, the more I walked with God the more I understood why obedience was such a heavy command to heed and why it was much greater than any sacrifice we could give unto God.

God gave us the ultimate sacrifice through His son Jesus Christ. There's nothing more we could give to equal that of His sacrifice unto us. Thus, our obedience to Him will always be far greater. Our yes is far more important than any loss we may deem great unto Him.

Obey God Through The Process

The story of King Saul always astounds me but when God led me to re-read his story in 1 Samuel before writing this book, I did not know why, but I simply chose to obey.

Now, I see what God's command was unto me.

> *"Do not become like King Saul in your obedience Priscilla, but trust me and obey me throughout the process. AKA wait for me."*

When Saul was anointed king of Israel by the prophet Samuel, he was given specific instructions regarding how to wage war against Amalek for ambushing Israel when they came up out of Egypt.

He was instructed by God to wipe out all of the Amalekites and save no one in the process. However, Saul saw fit to save the Kenites who had shown kindness to the Israelites and lived in the same city as the Amalekites. Additionally, after the massacre, he chose to set aside some animals that belonged to the Amalekites as a sacrifice unto God.

Saul was so proud of his actions and judgments in the process that He did not understand that what he had done was wrong. He had made a way for himself and also obeyed God. What could be better than that? You cut corners here and there, but never stray too far from the main task God called you to, shouldn't God be happy?

How many times do we think like this about ourselves when we are walking in obedience to God? It's not like anyone got hurt right?

In your eyes, you remain pure but still cut some corners. So what's the matter as long as you're not engaging in sex, drinking, or doing drugs?

Well, the fact of the matter is that you **chose** to disobey. For partial obedience is still outright disobedience, no matter how big or small. God is a *covenant-keeping* God, which means He will *not* remove his remnant to placate (ease) your indifferences.

We may struggle at times to understand the commands of God, but this does not mean that He changes them to gain our understanding. No! In fact,

He changes us to understand. Thus, even if a few are disobeying or obeying, God's will remains the same. Where we fall short is altering steps in His commands to fit our understanding and fill in the gaps as to where we "think" God went wrong or might have missed a step.

Samuel's rebuke did not fall upon the ears of Saul's understanding, but instead to his deeds and actions that he believed were transparent enough for all to see and understand. However, Samuel was not impressed by these deeds and neither did God. Instead, they were both distraught at the *audacity to sin and call it obedience.*

> "Then Samuel said, Do you think all God wants are sacrifices—empty rituals just for show? He wants you to listen to him! **Plain listening** is the thing, not staging a lavish religious production. Not doing what God tells you is far worse than fooling around in the occult. Getting self-important around God is far worse than making deals with your dead ancestors. Because you said No to God's command, He says **No** to your kingship." 1 Samuel 15:22-23 (MSG)

God used Samuel in the process to not only *anoint* Saul but to also *rebuke* him.

In reference to the prophetic voices discussed in chapter seven, there was one voice that did not lead me astray, but instead, it directed me in holy rebuke and called out my lack of obedience towards the voice of God. Nicholas Karinge (Nick) not only tarried with me but fought alongside me against the spiritual attacks that were being waged in and over my life's purpose.

Nick saw what I would become and beyond in the spiritual realm. He also knew that I had it in me to fight my own battles.

Being Seen and Seeing People

At this phase in my life, I still did not know what it felt like to be seen and what the proper response to that was.

Why was it so important that the God of all heaven, the creator of heaven and earth would stop still to speak to me? I felt as if I was wasting God's or Nick's time when they would prophesy over me, and I would rush or downplay the moment.

I had spent my whole life battling with being seen, and it played into my vulnerability issues. For example, in prophetic moments when God chose to speak to me through His people, it felt like quite an honor, but I still didn't understand why. I wrestled with understanding the reasons why He did not speak to me directly yet He has the power to. I also did not like the attention you got when you were prophesied over. It felt like a counseling session on steroids.

That being said, I knew of prophetic ministry and grew quite fond of it and its mystery. It felt familiar; almost as if it was second nature and something I could not avoid, but it was also off-putting in some instances. Looking back now, I believe I had been operating in that gift my whole life towards others but I shied away from it when it came to dealing with the inner parts of my soul.

Likewise, even if I learned to appreciate the prophetic ministry on my own, I was never taught how to cultivate and minister through it until God instructed my dad to plant a church in 2015, called Rhema Gospel Church.

The **vision** of Rhema was and still is to become a prophetic force proclaiming the living word of faith to the whole World. Furthermore, the **mission** of Rhema is to prepare God's people for service as a Kingdom of Priests and a School of the Prophets who are called to declare the love of God to the World.

Nicholas taught me how to usher in the presence of God on a deeper level and it's not to say that I wasn't at a good level. Yet for God to reveal the hidden things in my life and outline the path he had in store for me, there were levels of faith I needed to reach to receive what He had to say, all of it had to fall on good ground.

Therefore, how could I receive, or even believe the grandiose revelations over my life if I was still struggling to be vulnerable with people, God, and hear His voice audibly? I know God speaks differently to people. However, to me, it was a specific voice that I learned to tune into not only in my mind but in my heart as well to comprehend the message, He was delivering. In order to tune into that voice, I had to become vulnerable and sit with it in that space.

On the contrary, this voice did not want to manipulate me but set me free and it was eager about the process more than I was. God was doing a new thing in me, and He was patient with me even if I did not understand it.

I was learning to surrender through being vulnerable, have the courage to stay vulnerable, empathize with others, and most of all myself.

All of this taught me self-acceptance which enabled me to change my viewpoints of others and myself.

When you have a clear view of who you are, you can view others properly without feeling a sense of disdain in yourself.

As I have always told my young mentees, inspiration should never corrode your identity. You can be inspired by another individual and strive to emulate them but still maintain your own identity throughout the journey.

For example, I have been asked many times how living as an Akorino girl was like when I was younger living in the United States and even to this day. My answer is always simple. We tend to carry the personality and character traits we are born with as burdens throughout life. When in reality, these are **heavenly gifts** purposed by God.

God doesn't make junk nor does He place us here on earth to merely exist without a purpose. Instead, He uses these traits to highlight our differences and similarities at the same time. We are all human, but what we bring to the table is completely different. These differences allow us to achieve a common goal as well as learn from one another alternate routes towards that goal.

Even though we have opposing views, we all feel, we all think, and most importantly, we all have a desire to become the best versions of ourselves, even when we haven't begun the work. However, God is not intimated if you have or have not begun your journey, he formed you perfectly in **His image.** Nothing is missing or broken in you, as a matter of fact as He formed you, He was writing every part of your story as well! Wow!

Psalms 139:14-16 in the Message translation, is my favorite bible verse to refer people to when I explain my experience growing up not only as an Akorino but how not I but God intended it to be so. Therefore, not my will but His will be done on earth as it is in heaven. If he saw it fit to be so, then it is so. Now, this does not mean I coasted through life without questions, actually, I had many. However, when I stopped fighting my indifference, I learned to embrace this gifting:

> *"Oh yes, you shaped me **first inside**, then out; you formed me in my mother's womb. I thank you, High God—you're breathtaking! Body and soul, I am marvelously made! I worship in adoration—what a creation! You **know** me inside and out, you know every bone in my body; You know **exactly how I was made**, bit by bit, how I was sculpted **from nothing into something**. Like an **open book**, you watched me grow from conception to birth; **all** the stages of my life were spread out before you, The days of my life **all prepared** before I'd even lived one day"* Psalm 139:14-16 (MSG).

This verse brought rest to my weary soul when I would question my upbringing and compare it against society's expectations of me.

"You would be completely perfect if you had or showed your hair," they would say.

Even when I was peer pressured in the locker rooms or swimming pools to show my hair, I still felt as if something was missing. And it was my integrity or better yet lack of it.

I aimed to please others at the expense of losing myself and feeling guilty in the process. However, all of that shifted when I went through a one on one session with the best facilitator God single-handedly picked to walk me through this next season in my life.

One-on-one sessions came towards the end of the Life Transformation

School schedule also known as LTS. To give you a glimpse of LTS, here's their mission statement on their website.

> Led by Graham and Marie Catto, LTS is about your heart being won over by the unfailing love of the Father, moving into the freedom of forgiveness, aligning yourself relationally in humility and honor, and receiving the authority and position you have in Christ by grace. It's a lot more than information, it's an impartation of Father's love and humility. Each person will participate in a small group discussion as well as have a personal prayer ministry time devoted to them.

During LTS we would all explore these four significant questions:

- Who is God?
- What has God done?
- Who are we?
- How are we to live?

Growing up as a pastor's kid, concepts such as God's unconditional love as the central theme in our lives and how that plays out in our relationship with Him were already ingrained and exemplified by our parents from birth. However, as we grow in life, we tend to seek out the unknown and through that invite alternate voices into our lives with alternate choices. This then convoluted and skewed my perception of the Father.

Therefore, not only did I have to re-learn God's unconditional love for me and how that shaped my entire life, but I also discovered how understanding the love of the Father serves to deepen our relationship with others.

Additionally, LTS revealed to me how to live a *genuine* Christian life, unguarded and unreserved. This last part followed after the shift that took place during my one on one session.

I always joked with my friends about what would happen if they made me remove my kilemba (turban) during the session. Oh my goodness, you better have your hair washed and combed right. *To my natural 4c (hair type) sisters out there, you all know the struggle!*

As much as I joked and more, God definitely had something up His sleeve. During that session, we sat there together in silence waiting for the Holy Spirit to reveal the work He wanted to do within me. It was not long before I was confronted with my worst fear.

"I feel led to have you remove the turban."

Immediately, I wanted to shout Heresy! Lies! God would never ask such a thing! As the anger and offense stirred in my soul, I was met with an unnerving calm to *surrender.*

It's almost as if the Holy Spirit placed His hands over my mouth and beckoned me to sit down. Internally, the struggle that seemed to war within forever, faded in an instant. In the blink of an eye, I was back to normal and so I obeyed and began to remove my turban nervously.

I felt as if I had been asked to undress in front of a crowd, and that is exactly the message God was trying to use. If God would give us His Son to have us in return, why was I afraid to trust Him?

I sat there feeling naked and afraid my facilitator pursued me with questions that tore into my soul.

"Why are you so afraid... What are you afraid of... **Why are you so ready to go back?"** Her words resounded clearly, peeling back layers of my heart.

Back to what, you ask? The comfort of what I thought was my only identity. I had made my turban the center of everything, even exalting it above God and it was evident in my uneasiness. I felt as if I was sinning or breaking a law that I had assumed my parents had set forth. God was revealing to me that, yes, this was a piece of His glory in my life, but it was not the Highest glory.

In fact, it was not the turban that would get me into heaven because if that was the case, the whole world would be covered in them. This obscure perspective was filled with pride and ego of self, that I held the key to my salvation.

My father and mother never instilled that in me. No, they in fact instilled the opposite: we do this in obedience to the Father and what He has called us to do to *"be ye separate."* Our separation does not make us special. It is an act of our obedience to stay separate and unique amidst the constant temptation to rebel, conform to the patterns of this world, or stray from the covenant made with God.

This turban is a reflection of God's goodness in my life, and what He has called me to be in His eyes, not man. Wearing a turban does not reduce or increase the love God has for anyone else and He may ask of you to make a covenant with Him for something specific such as not wearing jewelry or pants or etc. God's ask of you should not be used to shame others. If He did not ask them and place that desire within, let them be.

So to bring it all back into perspective, on that day, I learned that God would not have any other God before him and that there was more to me than the turban. I was Priscilla—a woman, a daughter, a cousin, a friend, and a colleague. I was black, I had brown eyes, although, to some, they swore I wore contacts. I was a good singer, a good dancer, and oh, I was Akorino.

LTS taught me to embrace the gifts God had given me and to surrender what I deemed to be a burden unto God. In doing so, I invited Him into my process of **BEcoming** and we walked side by side, as He miraculously revealed His truth through it all.

Once I owned that this is who I was in God and not man, the desire to show my hair or be who society wanted me to be, waned. I knew that my reward came from God, the Most High, not earth or below. If they came from below, there would always be an expectation that I would never meet.

For example, if I all of a sudden dyed my hair and put on rastas, there would be someone or a group of people saying I was misled. Better yet, backslid when they too were probably flaunting the exact same hairstyle I had.

I am not saying that changing hair or having the freedom to show it as you wish is bad. What I am saying is that with mankind, there is always an expectation to meet. However, with and in God, you are complete. You are whole. There is nothing else you need to fill.

I am truly thankful to my facilitator for being sensitive to the Holy Spirit and helping me navigate such a pivotal moment in my life.

I also want to thank Nicholas Karinge for being used by God to redeem the prophetic utterance in my life and highlight to me just how much God's children matter to Him. Glory be to God for sending **His** shepherds and prophets to aid **His** people.

9

Alone with God; Lessons from My Wait

Before our minds and hearts can perceive or receive what is happening in our lives, God is always in the background doing a new thing, even when we do not feel it or see it. The important thing to carry along is, faithful is He even in the waiting period, for He alone understands and *accepts* our frustrations. Remember, no matter what your emotions and thoughts tell you, they are not always correct.

> *"Meanwhile, the moment we get tired in the waiting, God's Spirit is right alongside helping us along. If we don't know how or what to pray, it doesn't matter. He does our praying in and for us, making prayer out of our wordless sighs, our aching groans. He knows us far better than we know ourselves, knows our pregnant condition, and keeps us present before God. That's why we can be so sure that every detail in our lives of love for God is worked into something good"* Romans 8:26-28 (MSG).

Even when they are correct, I always defer back to God for confirmation or clarity. You may ask, why is it that friends or family cannot save you or help you?

Well, it's not that they can't. Most of us are blessed to be surrounded by people who not only care for us but see beyond the limits we place on ourselves.

Over the years, I have put to memory the voices that I allow entrance into my life knowing with full confidence that they will lead me back to God for direction and even if they do not, doing so for myself has empowered me in spaces I never thought possible. Learn to recognize those voices in your life, and if you do not have them, having God is enough.

Take King David for example, when He was crowned the next king of Israel he spent years in the wilderness tending to his father's sheep. Prior to my season of writing, God instructed me to read David's journey in the wilderness, and the whole process it took to become king.

We tend to equate David as a friend of God, and a man after God's own heart, oh so confidently, but do we ever stop and question why he was so acquainted with the King of Kings?

As I surveyed the chapters, I did so with a fresh perspective to see what God was doing through David, even when he could not see it. The more I read, the more I cried and it wasn't the cute one teardrop rolling down your cheek type of cry. Instead, this was a deep weep, from the wells of my soul because I related to the turmoil, heaviness, and despair inside of David as he tried to comprehend as well as obey the will of God over his life.

How could God favor David with Saul only to have him relentlessly hunt David down in order to kill him? Plus, wasn't David to be the future king of Israel? Why would God move him from the proper training place of a king to the desert?

When would this trip to the wilderness and Ring-Around-The-Rosie battle with Saul end? There were many times in the story where David could have killed Saul, but he refused *out of respect* for the man that God had appointed King.

Likewise, David chose to extend grace and mercy towards Saul who finally confessed with these words:

> *"You are more righteous than I," he said. "You have treated me well, but I have treated you badly."* 1 Samuel 24:17 (NIV)

I am sure David's surrender to the process of becoming was not easy. For example, when he struggled to find his true identity as a young shepherd boy, that struggle humbled him and God used it to crown him the next king of Israel. God does not call the qualified; He qualifies the called.

Even when David felt *indifferent* among his siblings, his uniqueness and boldness were displayed to all when he defeated Goliath. Also, it gave him favor with Saul, and the musical gifts he developed in his season of waiting played an important role when Saul was troubled by evil spirits.

All of these traits that David may have carried or viewed as a great burden led him to triumph in every season as he learned to lean not on his own understanding but God's. You see David's *surrender* gave him access to rooms and tables he might have never sat in if he had neglected the wilderness season that shaped his becoming.

Along the way, David learned to hear the voice of God clearly and sat in that place of waiting until he was *directed* to move. He also mastered the art of navigating as well as maintaining various relationships with wisdom while running for his life. This is the part I could not imagine doing, but I am thankful that it is not by our grace or might but His alone.

One of the many Psalms I identified with during my season of being seated, surrendered, waiting, and becoming, was Psalm 13:

> "How long, Lord? Will you <u>forget</u> me forever? How long will you <u>hide</u> your face from me? How long must I <u>wrestle</u> with my thoughts and day after day have sorrow in my heart? How long will my enemy <u>triumph</u> over me? Look on me and answer, Lord my God. Give <u>light</u> to my eyes, or I will sleep in death, and my enemy will say, "I have overcome him," and my foes will rejoice when I fall. But I <u>trust</u> in your unfailing love; my heart rejoices in your salvation. I will sing the Lord's praise, for he has been good to me." Psalm 13:1-6 (NIV)

This all goes back to perspective and reality, we. We could say that David did the most in the wilderness and that he was an emotional roller coaster; especially reading his Psalms unto the Lord.

Although when you *lean into* his story, you begin to understand and see things from his perspective. Take into consideration what it would have been like running from a madman who once favored you, and having multiple chances to kill him out of frustration but instead choosing to surrender your will unto God every time.

How exhausting! When we read the story from this lens, we begin to empathize and when empathy is present healing begins to take place.

Sympathy, however, looks on from the other side of the street saying *"oh my, that does look bad,"* while empathy *crosses* the street to assist even if it means being seated, surrendered, and present to hold space.

There was a season in my life, where God was all I had, and although I resented the people in my life for not seeing that I was alone. God used it to draw me closer to Him.

Just like David, God had not abandoned me, but he was pressuring me for the days to come when I would be surrounded by all types of people, voices, and choices. The discipline you are enduring momentarily is the training ground for you to determine your outcome, behavior, and most of all the heart posture for when the real test comes.

*"Will you lean on the voices of people when you receive such influence or will you remind and **abide** in Me?"*—God

This was the question God was asking me and the real answer would be revealed on the training ground, not the test, as I had thought. God will check your heart's posture even when He has called and prepared you to do His will.

He will not launch you into the battleground before you are ready, which is why the pressure from the training is better than test day. When you are testing, you may feel nervous, but you already know how to navigate the upcoming season because you were doing so alone before anyone was watching.

Thus, let God preserve you until you are ready to serve the world. The oil (anointing) which you carry is precious, and He does not want to waste it. Sons and Daughters, allow God to *complete* the good work in you.

As I waited upon the Lord and got trained in the wilderness season, He reassured me time and time again that only He could be my guide through the next season I was about to enter. In fact, no one had done anything wrong. **He wanted me to stay with Him until it was time and so He was responsible for not allowing any new relationships to enter my life for a good while.**

This specific season was tough, especially when I witnessed my friends and siblings navigating greater heights. I would often ask myself, am I just being lazy or am I waiting upon the Lord? I know I heard him, but was that really him or my mind pretending to be Him? This confusion set in my mind heavily when I sat in places of opportunity and growth.

I knew I was allowed to be there to *sit* and learn but not to act on it. God led me to these spaces, and he assured me that even if I was being inspired and challenged, my time would come.

This season was purposed for me to learn from others and gain new knowledge but do so while being seated, surrendered, and waiting upon the Lord. Look, I was tired of being seated, but the more I sat, the more I began to do so from a place of divine *rest*.

I did not have to act or perform for my place because God was already setting it up for me. My job was to simply *"be still and know that He is God"* Psalm 46:10 (NIV).

God always goes ahead to prepare a good place for you without lack, worry, or fret. As I wrote that last paragraph, I kept hearing God say put the word fret after worry.

"Aren't these words similar?" I wondered in my head.

"Google it!" He said.

Yeah, sometimes our conversations flow like that—very direct and mixed with a little attitude. So what was the result of my extensive research regarding worry and fret? Well, it was actually quite simple but deeply profound.

According to Google:

- To worry is to: *"give way to anxiety or unease; allow one's mind to dwell on difficulty or troubles."*
- To fret is to: *"be constantly or visibly worried or anxious."*

Subsequently, God wants us to completely remove our minds from the state of constant worry: fret. He understands the cycle it can keep us in, and wants to break it before it even starts.

Therefore, do not allow your mind to dwell on the constant repetition of how things could be or should have been. The real freedom that is gained from releasing what we think we know is much greater and sustainable, than the false freedom that comes from holding onto a plan built upon a foundation of worry and fret.

Now, for those thinking, *"well this is odd Priscilla... why would God the Father talk to you like that?"*

Earlier, I stated that we tend to complicate God. If and only if, this was your thought process here, I want you to ask yourself why? Surrender what you think you know to gain insight into what you do not know.

When we learn to enjoy our Heavenly Father, and He enjoys us, we form a lasting relationship that creates a pattern of its own. For example, you may talk to your earthly father in a certain way that adds humor to the conversation. Similarly, I talk to my Heavenly Father with humor.

God wants us to be open with Him, and in turn, He is open with us. He will not do what we do not require Him to do, God is a perfect gentleman. Most of all, He is the expert of "holding space" for us during our moments of confusion, loss, and or abandonment.

God is so trustworthy that when we make a covenant with Him, he is faithful to uphold our part even when we do not. He patiently waits for us to fall back in line and surrender our ways to Him. He will not move if we do not, He is patient with us and ever so kind.

> "God makes everything come out right; He puts victims back on their feet. He showed Moses how he went about his work, opened up his plans to all Israel. God is sheer mercy and grace; not easily angered, he's rich in love. **He doesn't endlessly nag and scold, nor hold grudges forever.** He doesn't treat us as our sins deserve, nor pay us back in full for our wrongs. As high as heaven is over the earth, so strong is his love to those who fear him. And as far as sunrise is from sunset, He has separated us from our sins. As parents feel for their children, God feels for those who fear him. **He knows us inside and out,** keeps in mind that we're made of mud. Men and women don't live very long; like wildflowers, they spring up and blossom, But a storm snuffs them out just as quickly, leaving nothing to show they were here. God's love, though, is ever and always, eternally present to all who fear him, Making everything right for them and their children as they follow his Covenant ways and remember to do whatever he said." Psalms 103:8-18 (MSG)

So, what was the greatest lesson I learned from being seated? The more I sat still, the more I learned how to listen, and be vulnerable with myself and others. Likewise, I learned how to do so from a place of empathy and not just sympathy. This was hard!

Empathy vs. Sympathy

We do not realize how much of the phrases that we use in times of discomfort are actually more sympathetic than empathetic. Here are some common phrases.

- *"Man, that sucks!"*
- *"Oh wow, that is terrible!"*
- *"I couldn't imagine!"*
- *"Well, I am praying for them; that is all I can do!"*

These are a few of the various types of phrases used to denote comfort in the midst of pain and most of all discomfort. All these phrases do is separate the person feeling the pain or loss from the ones who are not as if those without pain are the "normal" ones.

Since when did we begin designating pain or discomfort as being abnormal? We have been doing this for centuries now and it's displayed in our music, social media, and so much more. Having it all together and not displaying the "bad days" is more glorified because bad days or loss signify discomfort in some of us.

However, Dr. Brené Brown is an advocate for sitting in the places of discomfort to glean from growth. When we do this in ourselves, we are able and comfortable enough to do so for others.

> "Empathy fuels connection, while sympathy drives disconnection"
> —Brené Brown

Handpicked Individuals

I have worked in the Healthcare sector for over seven years now, and my time here has been an amazing journey towards growth. Some days have been tougher than others, but I can proudly say that each day is fueled with joy and laughter, thanks to one of my cherished supervisors.

Their mind is always going and moving to the next phase of things and this character trait has worked well alongside my scatterbrained self. They are able to draw out the creative side and make sure that the work you choose to do impacts you first before it impacts others. One thing I have admired is the resiliency throughout the years and how they have adjusted and molded us as a team to fit the season ahead of us especially when we did not expect it.

When the COVID-19 pandemic initially took place, our field became the center of attention. During these unprecedented times, our leaders made sure our work would still matter even if it looked different. We would lean into the discomfort and find that area of growth within ourselves to fight back; she was confident in us that we would succeed.

All of these accomplishments as a team were fueled by a leader who empathized with us during the shifts in workflow. When we did not understand a change, they connected to that pain and empowered us to find growth within the change; even if it was hard. It is now a year later, and we are still making strides and impacting our community.

A few additional individuals I believe God handpicked to usher me into this season of writing my story were my leaders in my line of work as a Community Health Worker.

They all worked hand-in-hand in different yet similar ways to usher me into growth as a professional and as an individual. I am humbled by their generosity and endless pour into me mentally as well as emotionally.

In life, there are people who just get you, and it's effortless, almost as if they have always been there. I can recall sitting in my office with one of them for hours, crying and expressing the deepest parts of myself, knowing that they were able to handle it.

We've shared this connection from the beginning of time, and it has grown over the years into a solid safe space for me. Even now, we joke about how it 'just happened.' We can't remember how or what or even when.

I have grown to revel in my uniqueness at work and not feel 'grounded' for it through my leaders. We all firmly believe in the idea of celebrating people and making work an environment to be seen for who you are, not just to be heard. You can be heard, but not make an impact because people never truly *saw* you.

When we see people, we do not just see their outward appearance, but we see their soul. We see the gifts, and talents they bring to the table; the impact they leave when they depart the room as well as when they enter. All of these things play a role in understanding who and what we are to the environment around us.

Thus, my leaders have always made sure we know just how much we not only mean to them, but to the team and organization as a whole. This is important for some people who may feel as if they are just a single piece of the puzzle when in fact, without that piece, the puzzle wouldn't be complete.

Pivoting During Change

Perspective is all about where you are standing in the moment. What do you see? Why do you see it and how do you see it? Since our passions are very similar, having that fuel to lean on with my leadership is a blessing in many ways, especially when the challenge to express my vision clearly can become a burnout.

Most importantly, my leaders have taught me how to hold space and let people be seen as they are no matter how difficult it can be to behold them at times. They have taught me how to pivot in times of struggle and find the route of growth, even if it means that I am the only one choosing to move forward.

Maintaining consistency in relationships is key, and so you must learn to pivot towards mercy until the necessary steps to withdraw yourself become the only option. Pivoting means finding alternate routes towards growth.

For example, boundary setting, active listening when you feel like you are about to respond in anger, perspective seeking instead of being assumptive and judgmental. Overall, these routes should not be offensive or cause harm to anyone but instead cultivate an environment of respect for one another.

On the other hand, the act of pivoting can be mentally and emotionally exhausting at times, especially when we have trained ourselves subconsciously or consciously to respond from a place of defense, ego, pride, and or not respond directly through passive-aggressive acts.

In order to pivot correctly, we have to surrender the preconceived ideas that we know other people's stories best. But how do we do that when we hesitate to acknowledge our own stories? How do we hold space for another person, when we do not even know how to do so for ourselves?

For some, the experiences from the past and or present are sometimes too intense to address. For others not so much. Through it all, we can learn to be a safe haven for one another.

In the next chapter, we will journey through owning your own story and what that means. Dr. Brené Brown discusses this in her book "Rising Strong" stating that, *"you either walk inside your story and own it, or you* **stand outside** *your story and* **hustle** *for your worthiness."*

A moment of silence here for those that feel like they just got the air knocked out of them.

Deep breaths, in and out.

Let's continue.

10

The Art of Living; Being Seated

My transition into adulthood was quite the trajectory. Internally, I felt different or misunderstood as an individual.

Have you ever felt misunderstood at some point in your life?

Allow me to set the scene of the house I grew up in before I expound on being different.

My father, whom I mentioned earlier, is a pastor, and a university professor. He received his Ph.D. in Religious Studies from Baylor University. My mother is a nurse and a skilled businesswoman who knows how to successfully negotiate any venture placed before her. My older brother is an economist with the World Bank and a thriving entrepreneur.

My older sister(second-born) is a nurse as well and an assistant professor/public health program director at her local university. As you already know, my educational experience is focused on psychology and mental health. Furthermore, I am a Nationally Certified Counselor and a licensed practicing associate.

Without my family's consistent correction, guidance, and encouragement, I would not have had the courage to push through the painful moments of denial or the public's constant speculation of what I was doing with my life.

Author's Note: The mental and emotional struggle it took to realize that my family was for me and not against me, was a strenuous one.

On the other hand, it released the necessary fruit in me to not only encourage but to sit, listen and hold space for those who encountered the same struggles of identity within.

Now that I have laid the foundation of who my family consists of, let's journey through the household I grew up in.

The Root Problem

In my family, our core values are God first, family second, and education third. This is the main reason we moved from Kenya to the United States. I remember receiving the news from my mother, but little did she know that I already knew.

God is so kind, and so special that He made a way for me to experience my father close by even when we were miles apart. Every night, I would dream of my father swaying me back and forth on a swing set as he told me about his day, then he'd ask about mine. He'd also tell me any exciting news that he had to share that day such as the day he would come to visit us back in Kenya, as well as the day we would all go back with him to the United States of America.

Soon what seemed to be a short time abroad for studies, turned into a lifelong adventure for us all. The day my mother found out that I knew of this news, she stared at me in disbelief pondering when, who, where, and how.

Thankfully my mother's faith in the Lord was strong as she soon began to connect the dots and trust that I was safe in His hands to understand the mysteries of the Lord. I never questioned it or doubted it, my faith was strong as a young girl and I knew that it was God and God alone who would tell me such news through my dad. I just knew.

As we explored this new land of opportunity, we made sure that our home always felt like home (Kenya) no matter where we were in the world. My parents worked hard to ensure that we lacked nothing as they created a positive adjustment and experience for us as children.

Pause.

Ring the bells and sound the alarms because I want to applaud the immigrant parents and children around the world.

Allow me to commemorate the way you navigated the pressures to learn a new culture, language, currency, and so much more with such resilience; now, that is admirable. In addition, you still managed to hold high the maintenance of your own cultural heritage while adapting daily to a new lifestyle. Every day is a delicate dance between acculturation and assimilation to find one's identity in this foreign land.

I am thankful to bear the fruit of it and I hope that we as children of immigrants, will continue to pass down the legacy of our parents to our children as well as their children's children.

I saw firsthand the struggles my parents faced to find a solid foundation for us as a family. Whether that was a place to worship that aligned with our beliefs, a good school district, and even a place to live that was safe for us all.

It was not long that things began to fall into place and a stable routine quickly followed suit. During the week, it was wake up, school, homework, sleep, and repeat. On the weekends, we took trips to the museums, libraries, and went to church on Sundays.

My parents eventually found a "tribe" that they could call family and reach out to in times of need. This group became the safe space my parents needed to fill the void that arose from time to time and help them walk through difficulties that affected us as an immigrant family.

Furthermore, they found within their friendship, a group of people who listened consistently from a place of empathy, not sympathy. To this day, those relationships still exist.

Although the good times were many for us as a family, in the midst of all this, I was left to navigate who I was within this new culture, and not only that, I left to find my own tribe. It did not matter if they looked like me or not, but what mattered was a safe space to belong and be seen for who I was. It was what I hungered for more than anything.

I watched my older siblings who were closer in age adjust quickly with one another, as they excelled in their studies, social relationships, extracurricular activities, and so much more.

Throughout my high school, undergraduate, and graduate studies, I consciously assumed that their adjustments had been easy. With this perspective in mind, resentment fueled inside of me each time they succeeded whether at a social or academic achievement; the fact that they succeeded was enough to throw me into fits of rage.

As I was struggling to find my identity, process the world around me, and others; success after success was their song. However, all of that changed when I began to comprehend what being seated meant in my personal journey, what surrender required, and most of all, leaning into the discomfort when things became unmanageable mentally.

The more I confronted my cognitions and emotions, the more I began to understand why they had been wired in such a way and how I had given this way of thinking permission into my life.

My mental and emotional instability was the result of files/tapes filled with false truths replaying themselves in my head. These false truths were the consequences of the unanswered questions I had towards my family, friends, and society.

I was left to create false biases to make up a world that I already didn't understand fully. I was embarrassed and deeply saddened the day I realized that my assumptions towards my brother and sister growing up aligned with specific groups of people in society who had *already* written them off whether it was based on the color of their skin, accent, academic achievements, or etc.

As I listened to their experiences on my sister's podcast, *Talks With E,* the episode titled *"Let's Talk Racism: A Man's Insight,"* I was stricken with grief, shame, anger, and guilt. Even after the freedom juice that Dr. Brené Brown's Ted talks and books had fed me, shame took precedence, and immediately the temptation to walk away from vulnerability beckoned loudly.

As my siblings shared story after story, I was confronted with two huge waves of truth on two sides. One half was the truth that had been clear to me from the beginning yet jealousy had tainted my soul and blinded me to it.

The other half was real, pure, raw truth and this truth hurt the most because it was the one that I did not want to see, but in my blindness wished for it. I recall turning the talk off early because the truth that was downloading into my psyche was too much to bear.

As I sat there sinking into what felt familiar, I felt like I was in the movie Get Out during the scene where he was just floating into the depths of his soul or psyche. All in all, I did not know what to expect but what I did know was that this out-of-body experience was just too much for me.

A deep void appeared in my soul that day and I quickly became apathetic to the world. Without any mental, emotional, or spiritual solace, I sat in my room frustrated and confused for a few days. I went from blazing hot with fury to a fire within that burned blue and filled me with shame. I knew that this wasn't the right response, but shame would not help me heal nor would moping around my room, but with everything else taking place in the world, who could focus on one thing at a time? It was all too much to bear, but in hindsight, who *told* us that it was ours to bear?

> *"Cast all your anxiety on him because he cares for you."* 1 Peter 5:7 (NIV)

As the world echoed with discussions of police brutality, racial inequality, privilege, mental health, health care, Covid-19, and more, I did not know who to turn to, and I could not divulge the mental rollercoaster I was going through to just anyone. I needed to be wise in my pursuit, especially at the expense of my siblings' character. Protecting them was key before addressing my emotions at least that is how I wanted it to be.

You may be thinking, wasn't this my experience to a walkthrough? Yes, it was. Wasn't this my truth to share? Yes, indubitably it was. However, just because it's yours to share, assassinating people's character as you tell your truth is unnecessary—no matter how badly you feel treated.

I say this because I wanted to maintain my siblings' image back then, and make it clear that they had done *nothing wrong to me* or towards me. Even to this day, I will always protect their image because to me, family always comes first and I am blessed to walk alongside such siblings.

The path I took to avoid this blessing of having such amazing siblings was long, lonely, and treacherous. On the other hand, here I am still seated, still surrendered, and now, I revel in the place of belonging that God has set before me. He alone had been the One preparing me. He deserves the glory and the honor for my growth.

I had let the suppression of my emotions bleed into my mind and cause me to project mentally what I did not want to express verbally. One way or another, what you keep hidden and locked up inside will reveal itself.

For some, it is a gentle and slow decline, but for others, all it takes is one wrong word, glance, or tone to make you question if this is the same person you were talking to minutes ago.

Discerning the truth from lies becomes very difficult when you let jealousy blind you. In such instances, even the purest of hearts look like enemies of progress, while the real enemies of progress are perceived as pure in heart.

Therefore, do not let your heart become troubled, confused, and unruly to the task God has ordained you for. When you rush to be seated, you forget to maintain the lessons ahead of you that brought the table to you, and instead, you focus on bringing the table to yourself. This is no act of surrender. *(Further explanation later)*

Following the first episode, I made a conscious effort to tune into the next episode of the podcast that my siblings titled *Part 2: Let's Talk Racism: A Woman's Insight*. This series was by far my favorite.

It included a few of my favorites sharing their experiences of what it meant to be a woman in this era and all of the various barriers that women encountered day to day; specifically women of color.

Everything they said left me speechless but one profound statement that left me in tears was *"if I can leave you **feeling a sense of empathy** not just for me but for humanity as a whole **through my story**, then I have **accomplished** my mission."* Talk about an emotional punch to the gut again.

That week after, I decided to disconnect from the world of social media completely and give myself the safe space to properly address the mental and emotional state my heart and mind was in as I replayed my siblings' experiences with race and culture alongside the personal assumptions I had created of them.

As I reflected over the few days, months, and years, Dr. Brown's statement of what it meant to **own your story** came to my mind over and over:

> "You either **walk inside** your story and **own** it, or you **stand outside** your story and **hustle** for your worthiness."

Unknowingly, the "hustle culture" was part of what had launched me into a spiral of depression and despair. I had somehow felt *obligated* to be invited to the table, and when I found myself seated there for once, I became arrogant to the fact that it was someone else's place instead.

During my disconnection from the social world, I learned that I had chosen to address the main problem, but not the **root** of the problem. The main problem was my assumption of people and the world alongside my ego that I had the answers to it all or that I could fix it all.

I had taken everything I learned in college and molded it into my world, and that was a major warning we had all received from our professor during the initial phase of our clinical rotations:

> "Do not take what you learn here into your world, that is not the same. It may appear the same but trust me, the roots are different. You may be correct in your intent and assumption, but the root may not be ready to be addressed. Lastly, it is not always your responsibility to point it out."

I never brought my authentic self to the table, but rather a copycat version of who I thought I was or should be. The table in this case was any conversation or atmosphere that I felt I had the best knowledge or input. In such situations, I felt the need to perform for my identity and conform to any labels that I thought people had given me.

If it was mental health, I was the one to call on. If it was dealing with youth, I was there. However, I only wanted to be there for the label, not the impact it would have on the lives of people who were desperate for a change in their lives. I cared less about the people being served and more about the picture that was used on the flyer. This did not mean I was rude to anyone, but my heart posture was and that spoke more volumes than any of my words could ever do.

Has that ever been you? Have you ever found yourself so focused on the labels, that you'd rather know who was who at the party and where without really being people-minded? Does the label that people carry matter more than who people really are?

This form of thinking left me stuck wading through the shadows of my siblings who *did not* know I was carrying this weight or that I secretly blamed them for it. They knew nothing and they still **chose** to be safe spaces for me to express my vulnerability from time to time. You see when you find yourself stagnated in a cycle of doubt and uncertainty about who you are, *labels* become comfortable. You barely have genuine concern about people because you are fixated on the labels they have. You quickly adapt to the feeling of being told who you are by other people and gladly receive those labels half-heartedly.

Permission To Flourish

Before I graduated with my master's, I was the queen of the kingdom called *"what do you think?"* During this season in my life, I had lost count of how many times I referred to that phrase and eventually, lost touch with the self-confidence to think for myself. I always sought permission for everything and unfortunately, I sought it from the wrong people. I craved acceptance and this made me get into situations I knew very well were not working for me.

As a result of this behavior, my grades were affected heavily and my relationships already lacked the depth or safe haven that I needed as previously mentioned. I remember attending study sessions knowing good and well that I did not study effectively in the same environments as my friends did.

I personally learned through difficult conversations with family and deteriorating grade levels, that I needed a dark, quiet, and bleak space to study comfortably. This may sound like an old, creepy, abandoned basement or a sewer—it's not—however, I do not think that falling into a sewer when I was younger played a role in my preference for comforting environments.

Ask me all about your sewer requests and the best places to study, I've got you! All jokes aside, I knew that my extroverted self could not stand the idea of such a place to study, but I had to make the sacrifice count.

Because I chose acceptance over my schoolwork and while others succeeded in their studies, I failed miserably. You are probably thinking why did you do this? What was your motive? There was no motive. When you are in the search for approval, emotions run high and critical judgment runs low.

When I would ask my classmates for their input about my study habits and if they were effective, I was usually met with *"of course, if we are passing then so are you."* However, I was not passing, but I somehow believed that I would and could if I kept on. I knew deep down, this was counterproductive and wasteful of all my parents' hard-earned resources to keep me in school.

Hustling seemed more comfortable than taking ownership of what was truly going on. However, my need for approval from my peers could never allow me to stand ground and stop attending their study sessions.

At this moment I would like to thank the University of North Texas's Eagle Commons Basement Library for their time and resources to help me execute the best grades ever during my undergraduate experience! *"UNT Eagles Fight Fight Fight!"*

If you know…you know.

You cannot own something without hard work, and that was what I was avoiding… I needed to own my story, my experience, and accept myself but I was not ready to put in the hard work that was necessary for that to happen. Moving through the pain associated with my past seemed difficult, even scarier than moving past it. The pieces of my story were many, shattered like glass and I did not even know where to start to piece them all together.

Hidden in the depths of my soul, were those fragmented pieces of truth, that instead of working through them, I chose to cover up with labels as a coping method of holding myself together. Instead of analyzing them to understand what had made Priscilla who she was now, I ignored their existence and chose to identify with the labels that made me feel good about myself.

Also, might I add that the sources I would go to for solace and advice never noticed my lack of confidence, and even if they did, they never challenged me to think for myself. Surprisingly, I went to them hoping that they would realize that I was troubled. I would wait for this conversation to come, but it was moved aside with the distraction of shopping, grabbing food, and or any other topic that subsided the discussion.

Any form of encouragement came from a place of sympathy rather than empathy. This created separation and that made it even more awkward to address. It became clear to me that the people in my life at that time, barely understood my struggles and if they did, they did nothing to help. From this moment on, I began to address my own problems alone with God first before others and in turn, realized the power of empathy.

From this moment, I learned a lesson that I hope you take away from me. Never allow people who have gotten comfortable with your lack of self-empowerment, to speak into your life from a place of empowerment. Do you hear me?

If they consider themselves a close part of your inner circle and are not able to notice a change in your behavior or speech, do they deserve a front-row seat in your life? Rather, surround yourself with people who like my father likes to say, *"permission you to flourish."*

The main guiding principles my parents referred to throughout our transitional seasons from high school to university and onwards into our careers was this:

> *"We believe that families are much more than groups of individuals. They have **their own** goals and aspirations. A family is an institution where every child and adult should feel that he or she is special and encouraged to pursue his or her own dreams; a place where everyone's **individuality** **is <u>permitted</u> to flourish**."* —Dr. Solomon Waigwa

'Okay Priscilla, what does it mean to flourish? How or where do I begin?' You may ask.

My understanding of flourishing comes from the lives and achievements of two people, Chadwick Boseman, and my sister-in-law, Cecilie Wachira.

The way Chadwick Boseman lived life to the fullest amidst the pain and discomfort he must have faced is inspirational, to say the least. To me, he is the epitome of flourishing.

In addition to that, he made it a point to *see* people as they were without labels or titles attached to them when he was the one and only King T'Challa. Yet, even in his kingliness, he managed to maintain a humble attitude that was oh-so captivating to the eye and most of all our hearts.

He made an impact in so many ways that for some simply seeing and knowing him as the Black Panther was enough to send a wave of intense emotion over them when they found out about his passing.

Most of all, his legacy lives on, and to see that he kept his circle small yet made a ripple effect is what I want to attribute my becoming process to when I think of what it means to flourish amidst the pain the process may bring.

When Chadwick passed on, only a small number knew about his illness, but **many** knew about his strength. This impact was not just because of the title or label that he held as an actor, but more so as a gentleman who properly understood what it meant to be *seated* and *surrendered*.

A gentleman who understood from a personal place what it meant to live life to the fullest, and flourish while doing so. He was a gentleman who knew how to stay seated even when he had the authority to get up in many rooms. Although when he did get up, he did so with immense humility, empathy, vulnerability, and most of all courage.

During his speech at Howard University in May of 2018, Chadwick engaged and inspired the graduating class to *savor* the moment they were in. To stop and take in the victory that lay before them before rushing towards their next attempt at success. He made it clear that without an understanding of what the previous lessons and seasons taught you. You weren't moving in purpose but in performance.

"When you are deciding on next steps, next jobs, next careers, further

*education, you should rather **find purpose** than a job or a career. Purpose **crosses** disciplines. Purpose is an **essential** element of you. It is the reason you are on the planet at this particular time in history."*—Chadwick Boseman

Likewise, my sister-in-law, Cecilie Wachira is the embodiment of flourishing through finding purpose in your career. Her story is awe-inspiring and many know of her in the limelight from that place, but very few know of her outside of it.

As a well-known professional photographer in the D.C metroplex and internationally, Cecile has not only taught me to be proud of the grandeur impact that one can make in society, but she has also taught me to remember the *intimacy* of being *hidden* as well.

It is by being hidden and taking time away from the spotlight that we can remain truly grounded in ourselves and most importantly God. When we shy away from this space, we begin to push against growth and fall further into pride.

Cecilie has shared a few personal stories where pride was a constant visitor beckoning her eagerly to take the win and move up in her field. However, because she stayed true to who she was, she did not push against growth, but instead surrendered to becoming, and disciplined herself to remain seated.

Although many in her field did play their cards well to be seen and transition up in life, humility's whisper remained a constant compass guiding Cecilie through her endeavors no matter how grand her sphere of influence became.

The more Cecilie remained seated and surrendered, the easier it became to wait on GOD. She understood that her decision to sit still, humble, and not perform to be seen in rooms beaming with influence was simply the grace of God active within her.

As a result of this, she was noticed by many without her even speaking a word or sharing who she was. Cecilie was invited to photograph presidents, their families, dine with the Bishop of Rome, work with international soccer leagues, and the list goes on. In sum, humility and surrender to God's will over her life granted her continuous favor.

You must remember that although this is intrinsic growth. It does not exclude God from the process at all. On the contrary, it relies on Him daily like the air we breathe and water to drink. God is the Ultimate Coach in your journey to becoming because He knows the best paths to lead you on and how the process will go overall.

Lastly, one cannot become without the Grace of God granting you strength to pursue each day. This is where that ego, pride, and performance comes in because you are wanting to be self-made in an instant when in reality that does not happen overnight.

You can strive to be all that you wish to be, but without experiencing and understanding what it means to be seated first, the inability to surrender to anything that invites growth will be impossible.

Additionally, the courage to be vulnerable towards the process will be rooted in pride or sympathy and not empathy. For example, believing that I knew all of the answers and could fix everyone which in turn, resulted in many broken relationships.

Therefore, allow God to use each one of these terms interchangeably to teach you along the way how to be courageous, vulnerable, and empathetic.

Likewise, you will begin to notice yourself grow in humility before God because you will realize that you cannot surrender on your own... It is hard. We are tempted daily to take matters into our own hands, but when we learn that our hands aren't the Master Maker's hands, that is where the invitation to journey towards becoming begins.

So, what will you do when you are tempted to move rather than sit, surrender and wait? Waiting does not mean that action isn't taking place. Please remember that. As a matter of fact, *a lot* of action is taking place behind the scenes as God is busy putting the pieces together for your good.

Remember King David in the wilderness tending to his father's sheep all day and every day? All of this was his preparation to be the next king of Israel.

Sitting does not mean that action isn't taking place, rather it means that your heart is at peace regardless of the situation in front of you. In other words, you aren't pacing back and forth with the anxiety to perform in a space that hasn't been prepared for you.

You will notice you are growing in many ways in the process of becoming. One of them being, when you find yourself at peace in the same environment that once tempted you to perform for your worth. You will look back and realize the ease of the situation now because you have learned to *sit, surrender, and wait* for what is rightly yours.

Remember King David showing grace and mercy when he had every right to be mad and get revenge against King Saul?

There will be no need to fight for any spotlight, justify oneself, or anything because you have surrendered yourself and the journey towards growth to God.

Your heart will have the courage to face the vulnerable moments that come along with empathy for yourself and others as you continue to flourish in becoming.

In closing, I write to you from a place of rest and confidence in God knowing that this book has touched your heart in ways I would deem impossible. As you read the pages of this book, I believe that God was doing something miraculous in and through you.

Look how far you have come by imagining all that you can become. Nothing is impossible with God. Nothing!

When I envisioned my becoming process, and what God had in store for me, this image of kings and queens kept coming to my mind.

I pondered "why Lord? Why?"

He told me "this is how I envision you all daily as my children, but it saddens me to know this isn't a vision for yourselves."

How can you be called children of *The Most High God*, and not live like so? Like the royal priesthood that you are? A chosen generation as proclaimed in 1 Peter 2:9?

> *"But you are a **chosen** people, a **royal** priesthood, a holy nation, God's **special** possession, that you may declare the praises of him who **called you out of darkness** into his wonderful light."* 1 Peter 2:9 (NIV)

He went on to share with me that during the coronation of any king or queen in any country, there has to be a bow of some sort to accept the throne—the rightful seat. Yet, many of us have lost our bow. And some of us do not even know what we are bowing to.

Many of us think we are accepting positions of kings and queens; however, those positions are not of God. The spheres of influence there are not in range with the knowledge of the word of God at all.

The blessings of maintaining your bow are many, like earning the keys to a new car, house, and more. You may be thinking Priscilla this is a little much, a house? A home to call my own? Really?

Yes! A home to call your own!

When God crowns you, he calls you HIS own and through that comes the direct inheritance as HIS child! Thus, the cattle on a thousand hills that He owns as referenced in the verse below becomes yours as well!

> *"Listen, my people, and I will speak; I will testify against you, Israel: I am God, your God. I bring no charges against you concerning your sacrifices or concerning your burnt offerings, which are ever before me. I have no need of a bull from your stall or of goats from your pens, for every animal of the forest is mine, and the cattle on a thousand hills. I know every bird in the mountains, and the insects in the fields are mine. If I were hungry I would not tell you, **for the world is mine, and all that is in it.**"* Psalm 50:7-12 (NIV)

However, even as inheritors of the Kingdom, God does not need or rely on our external gifts and or sacrifices to please him. Instead, He desires the internal offerings of our heart; the consistency of our surrender to Him is what sustains our bow.

Continuous surrender yields good fruits in us such as humility and honor.

These fruits strengthen our posture and empower us to stay seated at His feet, even when life becomes rocky. Especially, in the moments when it's easier to get up and move the table towards you instead of waiting for God's time to usher you towards it. *Remember: The table is where the bountiful meal of endless possibilities lies. It's the place where you explore, grow, and enjoy your becoming.*

Don't rush the assignment! In the same manner, a farmer tends to his crops carefully in season and out; all of his efforts are to make sure each one is *ready* in due season.

Consequently, when we refuse to maintain our bow, and hand over our ambitions to God, fruits of bitterness and resentment spring up instead. As a result, the internal and external judgments of self and others begin to decay our judgment as well as the path towards our journey to becoming.

What was intended to be harvested for people's nourishment now becomes disposable due to its lack of nourishment and taste. The point I am making is, your transformation is not just for you alone as mentioned before.

Alternatively, it is beyond you and crafted for many others who will look to you to discover about their becoming. God calls forth specific people to fulfill specific seasons, therefore do not be caught unaware of your season.

In closing, as you continue to proceed through your personal season of growth, remember to submit your bow unto God. Only He will be able to sustain this journey and keep you seated in perfect peace as you grow courageously, vulnerably, and empathetically.

So, take a deep breath in, release, and hold your crown steady.

Here's to becoming!

Notes

INTRODUCTION

1   (SST; Carstensen, Isaacowitz, & Charles, 1999)

2   (Urry & Gross, 2010) cited by Grossmann, Karasawa, Kan, & Kitayama, (2014)

THE EXAMINED LIFE

3   "How the Maasai Labelled Most of Kenya." The Standard. The Standard Group PLC, July 27, 2011. https://www.standardmedia.co.ke/home-away/article/2000039725/how-the-maasai-labelled-most-of-kenya.

4   "The Pacifist Presence in Kenya" (Gachanga, 2021).

5   Pentecost Without Azusa. A Historical and Theological Analysis of the Akorino Church in Kenya. Unpublished Thesis. Baylor University , USA . (Waigwa, 2007)

6   West, Thomas G., and Plato. 1979. Plato's Apology of Socrates: an interpretation, with a new translation. Ithaca, N.Y.: Cornell University Press.

7   "APA Dictionary of Psychology." American Psychological Association. American Psychological Association. Accessed January 29, 2021. https://dictionary.apa.org/projection.

8   "Definition Of SUBCONSCIOUS". 2021. *Merriam-Webster.Com*. https://www.merriam-webster.com/dictionary/subconscious.

9   Freud, A. (1946). *The ego and the mechanisms of defence*. International Universities Press.

10 Baumeister, Roy F., Karen Dale, and Kristin L. Sommer. 1998. "Freudian Defense Mechanisms and Empirical Findings in Modern Social Psychology: Reaction Formation, Projection, Displacement, Undoing, Isolation, Sublimation, and Denial." Journal of Personality 66 (6): 1081–1124. doi:10.1111/1467-6494.00043.

11 National Scientific Council on the Developing Child (2004). Children's Emotional Development Is Built into the Architecture of Their Brains: Working Paper No. 2. Retrieved from www.developingchild.harvard.edu.

THE WAKEUP CALL

12 Bravata, Dena M., Sharon A. Watts, Autumn L. Keefer, Divya K. Madhusudhan, Katie T. Taylor, Dani M. Clark, Ross S. Nelson, Kevin O. Cokley, and Heather K. Hagg. 2019. "Prevalence, Predictors, And Treatment Of Impostor Syndrome: A Systematic Review". *Journal Of General Internal Medicine* 35 (4): 1252-1275. doi:10.1007/s11606-019-05364-1.

THE ENEMY TO VULNERABILITY

13 Sigmund Freud, 1917, From *A Difficulty in the Path of Psycho-Analysis*
14 Sharf, p.34
15 (Sharf, 2008, p. 35)
16 (Sharf, 2008, p. 47).

THE DIFFICULTY IN VULNERABILITY

17 Sharf, R. (2008). Theories of Psychotherapy and Counseling: Concepts and cases. USA: Cengage Learning.
18 Sharf, R. (2008). Theories of Psychotherapy and Counseling: Concepts and cases. USA: Cengage Learning
19 Sharf, R. (2008). Theories of Psychotherapy and Counseling: Concepts and cases. USA: Cengage Learning *(p.337)*
20 Sharf, R. (2008). Theories of Psychotherapy and Counseling: Concepts and cases. USA: Cengage Learning (p.337)

THE CHANGE I NEEDED

21 Picciotto, Gabriela, Jesse Fox, and Félix Neto. 2018. "A Phenomenology of Spiritual Bypass: Causes, Consequences, and Implications." Journal of Spirituality in Mental Health 20 (4): 333–54. doi:10.1080/19349637.2017.1417756.
22 Picciotto, Gabriela, Jesse Fox, and Félix Neto. 2018. "A Phenomenology of Spiritual Bypass: Causes, Consequences, and Implications." Journal of Spirituality in Mental Health 20 (4): 333–54. doi:10.1080/19349637.2017.1417756.

About the Author

Priscilla Wachira is a Nationally Certified Counselor and a Licensed Professional Counselor Associate in the state of Texas. She holds a master's degree in Clinical Mental Health from Texas Women's University and a Bachelor's degree in Psychology from the University of North Texas.

She is passionate about community engagement, outreach efforts, physical and mental health education focused on empowering young adults across various cultures. Her research interests include:
  - Health Equity as is it relates to women's health.
  - Exploring barriers that affect emotional expression among different cultures.
  - Mental Health stigma within the immigrant community
  - Cultural stigmas regarding shame, guilt, and vulnerability specifically.
  - The measure of authenticity, courage, hope, and resiliency from various cultural views.

Priscilla is a firm believer that, "People begin to heal the moment they feel heard." This healing is the result of a safe environment (space) that is created with the intention of providing emotional healing and connection instead of judgment or shame. In sum, Priscilla is confident of this: "When we tell our stories, we rid shame of its badge of dishonor over our lives."

When she is not writing in her favorite dimly lit office full of candy and snacks, Reese's to be exact. Priscilla loves spending time with her family at their ranch in Texas, visiting close friends as well as youth group mentees, traveling, and exploring new cultures.

You can connect with me on:

🌐 https://iamseated.com

www.ingramcontent.com/pod-product-compliance
Lightning Source LLC
Chambersburg PA
CBHW072015290426
44109CB00018B/2241